THE
CYNIC'S
DICTIONARY

T H E
CYNIC'S
DICTIONARY

R I C K B A Y A N

CASTLE BOOKS

This edition published in 2002 by
CASTLE BOOKS ®
A division of Book Sales, Inc.
114 Northfield Avenue, Edison, New Jersey 08837

This edition published by arrangement with and permission of
William Morrow, an imprint of HarperCollins Publishers, Inc.

Drawn letters by Donald B. Poynter

Book design by Patrice Fodero

Library of Congress Cataloging-in-Publication Data

Bayan, Richard.
The cynic's dictionary/ Rick Bayan.
     p. cm.
1. American wit and humor—Dictionaries. I. Title.
PN6162 B35 1994
423'.0207—dc20   94-5472
                      CIP

ISBN: 0-7858-1713-1

Printed in the United States of America

To my mother's family,
the APRAHAMIANS,
whose sensitivity
and gentle innocence
led me to expect the same
from the world at large.
Alas, I still do—
despite all the evidence
to the contrary
presented in this book.

PREFACE

Nobody loves a cynic. His friends grow tired of his airy detachment and cutting irony. His colleagues find him peevish and aloof. Productive citizens chide him for refusing to lead, follow or get out of the way. His dog curls up in a far corner of the room, and heaves an audible sigh. Even Nature casts a harsh eye on the poor fellow: Medical studies have suggested that cynics fall prey to coronary mishaps at a rate several times that of the general population.

So why, you might ask, do I *willingly* don the black cloak of public curmudgeon and naysayer? Why write a dictionary filled with bile, spleen and other dark unwholesome humors? Do I not cherish my precarious health, or look forward to the ripe contentment of old age?

Of course, of course. Like most of you, I have no desire to be tossed on the compost heap before my time. But this book demanded to be written, and I did nothing to squelch it. It's here, and that's that.

The Cynic's Dictionary is my personal response to an age

that scoffs at virtue and nobility . . . that makes culture heroes out of strutting rock musicians . . . that prizes the ugly and the obscure in art . . . that turns men and women into carping adversaries, and bright collegians into undifferentiated corporate bureaucrats . . . that rewards greed and glibness . . . that tells us, through the dictates of "political correctness," what we are allowed to think and say.

On top of that, I'm tired of losing socks in the wash.

Let me assure you that I am not a cynic of the hard-boiled school—one of those narrow-eyed miscreants who view life through a noxious cloud of cigarette smoke. I am (as I suspect *you* are) actually a disgruntled idealist—a sympathetic fellow with a fondness for dogs and most children. What about the "cynicism" that crackles throughout my dictionary? Call it a romantic's disgust with the shabbiness and sham of a cynical age. I wanted life to be a melodious waltz, brimming with gaiety and bittersweet regret; the times have given us *rap* instead. I feel swindled . . . don't you?

I should point out that I am not the first to have written such a book. Its most distinguished predecessor, *The Devil's Dictionary* by Ambrose Bierce, has been warming the chilly hearts of cynics for nearly a century. It is a brilliant book and, naturally, an underappreciated one—at least among mainstream readers and critics.

In *The Devil's Dictionary* the acidulous Mr. Bierce took on all of humankind—perhaps even the entire universe—

as the target of his wrath. It may have been too much for him. Within ten years, at the age of seventy-one, the old gentleman pulled up stakes, trundled down to Mexico and, as legend has it, vanished from this orb while in the company of Pancho Villa's raiders.

My own intentions are a little less ambitious than Bierce's, but probably just as reckless. Like my predecessor I do my share of sniping at the gods, and I readily confess to tossing numerous brickbats at human nature. But mainly I have taken up arms against the modern era—its sacred cows, its unholy terrors, its irritating little gremlins. The age has slapped me on the face; with this book, I challenge it to a duel.

Many of my targets are, I am quick to admit, as broad as a barn and just as easy to hit. Lawyers, for example . . . or fast-food restaurants. What I've tried to accomplish is to distill the essence of the offending phenomenon into a few well-chosen words, and to give those words an ironic twist that will leave you chortling inwardly with satisfaction.

I have taken care not to single out any individuals for ridicule. This decision arises not only from a morbid fear of lawsuits but also from my conviction that most people are the innocent creatures of their genes and their times. Unlike some of our satirists I take no pleasure in the prospect of trashing hard-built careers and reputations, no matter how deserving they may be of the honor.

You will find me less charitable toward *groups*—the endless array of special-interest factions, corporate henchmen, jargoneering professionals, teenage barbarians, media tastemakers, smug connoisseurs, body snobs, mobsters, new-age mountebanks, turncoat humanities professors, politically ostentatious celebrities and other insufferable cliques that currently infest our republic. I am aware that groups are generally composed of individuals, but I also observe that membership in any exclusive club—whether of local plutocrats or obsessive rock-climbers—stimulates something provincial and repellent in our natures.

I don't stop at groups either. Throughout these pages you will see me malign a host of late twentieth-century horrors, follies, professions, diseases, business practices and bogus amusements—sometimes with savage indignation, but just as often with a playful and mildly indulgent wink. I give you our times on a hot-plate of wit, roasted and seasoned for your gustatorial pleasure.

What a vast, pretentious and perfectly ridiculous parade struts across the landscape! What ripe possibilities for satire! Let me goad the obnoxious, defend the defenseless, play like a cat with whatever smacks of folly, and attack bullies from the incomparable safety of the printed page. What could be more fun?

Despite the occasional bouts of burnout or satirist's guilt, I amused myself immensely by writing this book. I relished the prospect of skewering all those ghoulies, ghosties and long-legged *bêtes noires* that had been pestering me for so many years. It was a pleasure, especially for a professional writer of no-nonsense direct-response advertising, to *play* with words once again after a long day's work . . . to aim a righteous barb at something vile . . . to romp among the wild absurdities . . . to experience the happy surprise of a perfect paradox popping into one's consciousness . . . to shape each idea into a compact winged missile that would fly straight to its target.

Of course I hope you enjoy *reading* my book as much as I did writing it. Until now too many decent folks have been observing the scene, shaking their heads and growing crusty around the edges. I say it's time you were given a chance to strike back, to flick off the sundry insults to your senses simply by laughing at them. If my book produces a few chuckles at the expense of our times, it will have served its purpose.

If anything in my book offends you—and I'm sure there is something in it to offend everyone—please bear in mind that I've crafted my definitions the way a caricaturist sketches a face: with an eye to the possibilities for whimsical exaggeration. And if some of you wonder how I could be so unrelentingly *negative,* let me assure you that *The Cynic's Dictionary* is as much an elegy for old-fashioned virtues and pleasures as it is a diatribe against decadence.

Having said my piece, I now commend my book to your safekeeping. I hope you will browse through it often, share it with friends and colleagues, and spread the word. I won't require that you memorize any of the definitions, although you're welcome to do so. And remember: If you ever feel demoralized, overwhelmed, appalled or befuddled by the times we all inhabit, *The Cynic's Dictionary* should convince you that you are not alone.

ACKNOWLEDGMENTS

I wrote this book alone, under my own limited powers, despite the daily rigors of a demanding job, chronic eyestrain, fear of writing the unthinkable, and numerous other distractions. For my perseverance and reasonably good humor in executing this difficult opus, I humbly acknowledge *myself*. And I say to other aspiring scribes, daunted perhaps by the slim odds of finding a sympathetic publisher, "Write it anyway!"

Now for a minor confession. Despite my own singular efforts, I might never have pushed this book to its present state of completion without the assistance of those I name below.

Let me thank the good people who perused my definitions in the early going and gave me reason to hope that I was onto something: Dr. John O'Connor, Lisa Wright, Eileen Lederman, the Buist family, Donna Haney, the indispensable Weaklands (Allen, Pauline, and Christina), Barbara

Gilson, Gary Viskupic, Yvonne Piper, Glen Solosky, Jeanette Werner, and Bob Gaynor. Joanne Kowalsky deserves special mention for inspiring me to revive this project long after I had tucked it away in a manila folder. Thanks for being there.

I owe a further debt of gratitude to my gracious and superbly effective agent, Regula Noetzli, who I hope will forgive my tongue-in-cheek gibe at her profession on page 19. To Toni Sciarra, my spirited editor, I say thank you for taking me on, and for going over my manuscript with a light but knowing touch. (See, I remembered the second *for*.) Thanks, too, to Tim Hazen and the other staffers whose efforts helped turn my manuscript into an actual book.

Others, living and departed, have indirectly contributed to this book by helping to shape my peculiar mind and character. Let me first pay tribute to the *public school teachers* of New Brunswick, N.J.—especially the following, whose skill, kindness and encouragement this student will always remember with gratitude:

Mrs. Mason	Mrs. Umholtz	Mr. Segal
Mrs. Lacher	Mr. Seaman	Mrs. Marder
Mrs. Lynch	Mr. Zabolinsky	Mr. Hutter
Miss Leonard	Mr. Loughney	Mrs. Silber

Among those *writers* who, for better or worse, inspired the style and spirit of this book, I name these five as accomplices: Juvenal, Rabelais, Dr. Johnson, Ambrose Bierce and H. L. Mencken, whose scowling portrait on the wall behind my computer undoubtedly telegraphed some of the book's best definitions into my receptive brain.

There is simply no room to name the many *friends,* past and present, whose minds have influenced my own. So let me just say to them: You are remembered by this cynic more often and more fondly than you might expect—even those of you who passed out of my life during what now seems like an earlier geological age, before the seismic upheavals of the late 1960s.

These acknowledgments would not be complete without mentioning my father, Aris Bayan, who taught me to love knowledge; my late mother, Chaqué Bayan, who taught me to love goodness; my dear aunts, Arpiné, Nevart and Ruby; my cousins, Steven and Jane; my ever-young Grandma Sylvia; and *mon frère*, Dr. Gregory Bayan, who for so many years brightened the cozy nest that was our home, and who remains my friend-for-life.

Finally, a tender farewell to my uncle, Steve Aprahamian, a gentle and devoted family man of multiple talents and enthusiasms, who passed away unexpectedly the day before I was to write these acknowledgments.

ABNORMAL Occupying a point outside the shifting boundaries of social convention, like a same-sex couple before the 1970s or a twenty-two-year-old virgin today. Others now living beyond the fringe include rhyming poets, English-speaking cab drivers, solitary restaurant patrons, celibate celebrities, non-academics who read anything written before 1920, businesspeople who read anything written before last Friday, Japanese underachievers, American students who can locate Japan on a map, and anyone who still says *whom*.

ABSTRACT ART   Incoherent dabs of paint in which serious critics detect shadings of metaphysical doubt or alienation, when in fact the artist was simply suffering from the effects of an undigested meat loaf.

ACADEMIA   A chronic disease characterized by a compulsion to write lengthy specialized treatises in unintelligible vocabularies, for the purpose of rising in the esteem of those similarly afflicted.

ACCORDION   The hybrid offspring of an organ and a pair of bellows, sounding like a harmonica with a pituitary problem; the happy scourge of polka halls and ethnic weddings.

ACCOUNTANT   A dutiful book-balancer whose role within a corporation is to protect it from creative ideas. See also ZOMBIE.

ACID RAIN   Industry's revenge on nature for resisting its advances; a vial of caustic liquid tossed in the face of a beautiful woman.

ACTIVIST   One who latches on to a cause like a terrier to a mailman's pants; an energetic meddler whose efforts can be as tiresome as they are tireless.

ACTOR   A professional exhibitionist who manufactures emotions in a manner convincing enough to earn a living, generally by reciting the daily specials to restaurant patrons.

ACUPUNCTURE   Waiting for a cure on pins and needles.

ADULTERY   An alarmingly popular sin that, despite its name, appeals primarily to those in search of a second adolescence, or a third, or a fourth.

ADVERTISING A glittering trap baited with the promise of status, personal fulfillment, socially desirable breath or a more amusing sex life. Victims are invariably snagged by the wallet.

ADVERTISING COPYWRITER The Cyrano of modern scribes, bound by honor to conceal his identity while his scented words woo customers for inarticulate clients.

AEROBICS A bouncy form of music-induced exercise, often led on video by sinewy women with stalled movie careers; said to improve the cardiopulmonary fitness of those who survive.

AFFECTATION The attempt to boost one's social status by aping the mannerisms of a more prestigious class, as when white athletes greet each other with high-fives, or bourgeois celebrities appear on talk shows wearing hole-in-the-knee jeans.

AFFIRMATIVE ACTION Liberal euphemism for ''No male Caucasians need apply.''

AFRICAN ELEPHANT Ivory on the hoof; the unfortunate custodian of impressive dental works that have struck the fancy of man and thus secured it a place in history alongside flying reptiles and Phoenicians.

AGENT A street-smart wheeler-dealer who manages a stable of warm bodies, arranges profitable assignations and reaps a portion of the proceeds, generally without wearing a broad-brimmed hat.

AGENT'S FEE The tribute that art pays to commerce.

AGING A supposed ripening into wisdom that most Westerners attempt to delay as long as possible.

AGNOSTICISM The wavering faith of those who ask, "If God is all-powerful, why doesn't He have a stronger handshake?" The only rational attitude toward an unknowable Providence, and unfortunately the only one that denies its adherents the certainty enjoyed by believers and atheists alike.

AIDS The Black Death updated for the free-love era; a slow-motion epidemic that threatens to purge the world of its sexual adventurers, along with hemophiliacs, intravenous drug users, recipients of tainted blood, half the population of East Africa, and anyone else who gets in the way.

AIR-CONDITIONING An invention for sucking the warmth out of the sensuous summer air, so that we might shiver in July and work through the season without dreaming of hammocks or lemonade.

AIR POLLUTION The forced conversion of all city-dwellers into chain-smokers.

AIRPLANE A flying ship considered by most studies to be the safest mode of transportation, at least while it remains aloft.

AIRPORT A destination to which we proceed with haste so that we can glance at our watches for the next two and a half hours. When our time comes to voyage into the great beyond, we enter a long tunnel that leads to a circle of light (See NEAR-DEATH EXPERIENCE), where a smiling attendant directs us to the first-class cabin or the *other* place.

ALCOHOLIC Clinical term for a tippler in an age that no longer smiles at tippling; graciously enables the sufferer to exchange a personal vice for an incurable disease.

ALIENATION The demoralizing sensation of being an outsider among insiders; a malaise frequently experienced by adolescents, American Indians, elderly folks residing in a state other than Florida, and liberal arts graduates entering the business world as clerk-typists.

ALIMONY The sum of money a man is commanded to pay his ex-wife in exchange for the pleasure of having her live under a separate roof.

ALUMINUM SIDING Neat metallic sheets that, when applied to the sides of a dwelling, confer upon it the ambience of a colossal lunchbox.

AMBASSADOR A wealthy person exiled to an alien land for the purpose of throwing parties, presumably with the hope of extracting government secrets from tipsy natives.

AMERICAN DREAM A nebulous national catchphrase used religiously by campaigning politicians, most likely because it has never been defined and therefore means whatever the listener chooses it to mean: freedom . . . educational opportunity . . . a piece of property with a tract home on it . . . a small plumbing business of one's own . . . two cars in the garage, including one Buick . . . a personally narrated late-night commercial on the local TV station, with spouse and children smiling stiffly in the background . . . a banner year . . . relocation to a Tudor-style house with a tennis court and a Jacuzzi . . . hobnobbing with the mayor at the eighteenth green . . . three cars in the garage, including at least one Mercedes . . . going national, with plumbing franchises in twenty-nine states . . . a summer house on the lake, with costumed servants . . . a son at Babson and a daughter at Bard . . . one's face on the cover of *Fortune* . . . a listing in *Who's Who* . . . a private jet with an 18K gold-plated toilet . . . one's face on the cover of *Time* . . . a villa on the Mediterranean, site of periodic bridge tourneys with Omar Sharif and King Juan Carlos . . . one's face on the cover of *People* . . . an affair with a nubile actress who has been nominated for at least one Golden Globe Award . . . invitation to dinner at the White House . . . surviving a corporate takeover attempt . . . surviving Chapter 11 . . . surviving quadruple bypass surgery . . . burial in a family mausoleum with at least one commissioned sculpture of oneself at the entrance . . . inclusion on God's A-list.

AMNESTY A retroactive license to commit political crimes with impunity, esp. as demanded by well-heeled leftist agitators who wish to distinguish themselves from criminals without education or breeding.

AMUSEMENT PARK A walled city populated mainly by teenagers, who willingly pay to have their bodies and brains agitated on a variety of fiendish contraptions designed to induce vomiting.

ANCHORPERSON A bland, well-coiffed TV entertainer who is paid more to read the news than ten reporters are paid to report it.

ANGINA A sneak preview of greater heartaches to come.

ANGST A form of suffering caused by too much thinking; a phenomenon probably incomprehensible to anyone who owns a recreational vehicle.

ANHEDONIA The pathological inability to derive pleasure from shopping malls, overwork, urban squalor, indigestion and chronic lumbago.

ANIMAL RIGHTS A loopy, well-intentioned activist movement that, in its extreme form, harbors more compassion for a captive circus elephant than for the hapless trainer on whose face it sits.

ANIMAL SHELTER Death row for surplus dogs and cats.

ANOREXIC Exhibiting the alluring slimness of a skeleton, like the prose style of a minimalist writer.

ANTIHERO A spiteful slug whose utter lack of nobility endears him to a contemporary audience.

ANTIQUE SHOP A cluttered walk-in closet frequented by lovers of objects used by dead people.

ARRESTED DEVELOPMENT Prerequisite for success as a radio DJ or a social satirist.

ART DECO Fred Astaire's natural habitat, surviving to this day in a few urban centers where spire-topped towers still soar above the glass-and-concrete boxes. A screwball comedy in chrome and masonry, capable of whisking us back to an imaginary 1936 where Nick and Nora Charles are still chatting at the bar, and we absentmindedly collide with a leggy young redhead who flashes a wry Ginger Rogers smile. We know we've returned to the present when the redhead summons the authorities.

ART GALLERY A boutique for the merchandising of reputations, of which art is the incidental by-product.

ARTHRITIS A persistent headache in the joints; nature's way of rewarding those who have lived sensibly enough to attain an advanced age.

ARTIFICIAL FLAVOR A chemical concoction with the power to make grape soda taste more like grapes than grapes do.

ARTIFICIAL INSEMINATION Procreation without recreation.

ARTIST **1.** Anyone talented enough to win foundation grants and critics' kudos by making an impression at the right parties. **2.** Anyone who tweaks middle-class proprieties with the intention of generating free career publicity. **3.** Anyone with a recording contract. **4.** (archaic) A questing soul who pursues a singular vision, creates something of permanent value and dies with the rent unpaid.

ASPHALT The hellish black substance used to pave the earth so that it might be made safe for automobiles.

ASSASSIN A killer nerd with a sense of history; one who takes a shortcut to fame by sniping at the famous.

ASSEMBLY LINE The notion that if a job is worth doing, it's worth repeating 9,614 times a day.

ASTROLOGY An ancient pseudoscience and barroom conversation-starter founded on the premise that everyone born under the same stars will meet a dark stranger, receive a propitious business offer or suffer an attack of dyspepsia on the same day.

ATHEISM   A godless religion that retains all the dogmatic posturing of the faiths it so confidently denies, with few of the consolations.

ATOM BOMB   A poison mushroom that may be served simultaneously to several million unsuspecting guests; a quick cure for international political tensions and the common cold.

ATTENTION SPAN   One of the traits that formerly separated our species from the lesser apes; a capacity for prolonged concentration developed through centuries of scrupulous discipline, and zapped back to prehistoric levels with the invention of the remote-control switch.

ATTITUDE   A precision-crafted peevishness widely practiced by members of the under-thirty set, generally to elicit favorable hormonal responses from potential mates. Especially notable among rock stars and jeans models, whose sour faces aim at existential eloquence but more nearly suggest chronic bowel complaints.

AUDIOPHILE   A techno-snob who continually brags about his twenty-thousand-dollar stereo equipment, esp. if it produces frequencies only his dog can hear.

AUTHOR   A writer with connections in the publishing industry.

AUTHOR TOUR   A grinding, stress-laden two-week show-business gig for just-published litterateurs, some of whom might have to settle for posthumous fame.

AUTOEROTICISM A solo act generally practiced behind closed doors except by monkeys and a few of the more prestigious pop-music idols.

AUTOGRAPH A sample of penmanship freely given by the great to their awestruck admirers, and sold by baseball heroes to little boys. Also a commodity priced according to current tastes, which explains why a Marilyn Monroe fetches more than a President Monroe.

AUTO MECHANIC A grimy surgeon who operates in a garage and rarely loses a patient, although he sometimes performs unnecessary organ transplants to boost his income.

AUTOMOBILE A gas-guzzling horse on wheels; source of mobility for the masses, status for status seekers, exhilaration for the restless and sudden death for the unwary. Progenitor of suburbs, shopping malls, motels, traffic jams, BABY ON BOARD signs, drive-in funeral parlors and endless rivers of asphalt.

AUTO RACING A dozen daredevils going around in circles; thousands of cheering spectators waiting for a crack-up.

AVANT-GARDE The folks who design the emperor's new clothes.

AWARD SHOW A televised contest in whch the suspense builds as performing millionaires vie to see who can stage the most embarrassing spectacle. Winning techniques include gratuitous gushing, serial name-dropping, revealing more than the usual expanse of breast area (for either sex), or making self-congratulatory political statements on behalf of oppressed indigenous peoples.

BABY **1.** (pronounced BAY-bee) The object of a parent's adoration: a beloved bundle of bodily functions. **2.** (pronounced BAY-beh) The object of a rock singer's adoration: a beloved bundle of bodily functions unrelated to those implied in definition 1.

BABY BOOMERS A hip generation of perennial juveniles whose turbulent history commenced with ''The Howdy Doody Show'' and reached its zenith with the arrival of a spiky-haired saxophonist at the White House.

BACKLASH The inevitable gob in the face that greets any group spitting into the wind on social issues. The equal and opposite reaction to actions on behalf of women, minorities, political correctness, jogging, spotted owls, oat-bran muffins and other timely causes, sometimes legitimate, that have been marketed to the public with fatally obnoxious zeal.

BACKSTABBER Key corporate position for an aggressive self-starter who intends to rise to the top. Candidate must demonstrate aptitude for slandering colleagues while projecting an image of selfless concern for the organization. Report directly to upper management. Oral skills highly desirable. Excellent financial rewards and growth potential.

BACON What male providers used to bring home until it was deemed both carcinogenic and harmful to the sanctity of one's arteries; dietetically correct working couples now strive to bring home the arugula.

BAD BREATH A noxious blast of freshly exhaled air, conveying the rich scent of multiplying bacteria or semidigested food to our helpless olfactory organs. An offense we tolerate in dogs but revile in our close friends and colleagues, which explains why certain individuals on dates may be seen hyperventilating furtively into their own cupped hands.

BANK Where money automatically increases in value, especially when we need to borrow some.

BANKRUPTCY Exhaustion of resources by an individual, a company or a society, following a period of carefree dissipation. The first two may skip town or seek refuge in Chapter 11; the third is usually out of luck.

BARBARIAN Member of a vigorous, rough-mannered horde that delights in the destruction of advanced civilizations; e.g., the Goths in Rome, the Spaniards in Peru, and teenage street dudes in cities across the American republic.

BARBECUE A suburban summer ritual at which the eldest male of the household presides over a burnt offering that's undercooked on the inside.

BASEBALL A beloved American pastime graced for over a century by men of mythic stature; a game still played throughout the soft summer evenings on spacious green fields, where the eager spectator may watch young millionaires spit tobacco juice, throw tantrums and adjust their crotches in public.

BASEBALL CARDS Pocket-sized portraits that may be hoarded, gambled or traded at the discretion of the owner; notable for teaching our youngsters that some men are worth more than others. Once the currency of American boyhood, slowly amassed with nickels, dimes and street sense; now chiefly a speculative commodity exchanged among fanatical dealers who used to be boys.

BASKETBALL Dribbling for dollars; a fast-moving gymnasium sport good-naturedly devised by white men as a showcase for the superior talents of their black brethren.

Beautician   A professionally schooled hair sculptress whose own coiffure should be sufficient to scare off potential customers.

Beauty   An aesthetic radiance that delights the soul; a quality much admired in women, landscapes and tropical fish, but curiously out of favor in art throughout the modern era.

Bed and Breakfast   In Britain, a cheery and inexpensive lodging-place that astonishes travelers with monumental helpings of toast and marmalade, cereal and cream, sausage, bacon, eggs and grilled tomatoes. In the U.S., a pricy sleep-in antique gallery managed by polite neat-freaks, married or otherwise coupled, who shrewdly feed their guests oat-bran muffins in the hope that they might survive long enough to return next year.

Beeper   A portable electronic alarm used to summon indispensable professionals during their off-hours; e.g., physicians on the golf course or teenage drug potentates in the classroom.

Beer   An intoxicating golden brew that reemerges virtually unchanged one hour later.

Best-Seller   What a book is called when as many people buy it in a year as fill a stadium for a single University of Michigan football game. If a book's prose style is stronger than its publicity, a more fitting analogy might be a Swarthmore football game.

Bible Belt   The empire of the saved: a broad swath of land that sweeps from the Confederacy to the high plains, embracing all manner of Baptists and Methodists, revivalists and Holy Rollers, who gather to praise the Lord and dream of a place by the Beautiful River, until a tornado flattens their tent and they dream no more.

BICYCLE Formerly the chief mode of transportation for the prepubescent, exhilarating them with newfound joy and independence; a pleasure now appropriated by a clannish breed of quasi-professionals, who read specialized magazines so that they might acquire the bicyclistically correct helmet, water bottle, stretch pants and thirty-seven-speed Italian racer.

BIG BANG The primordial slap on the backside of the newborn universe; a theory astronomers have sought to rechristen with a more suitably dignified name. This lexicographer humbly suggests Harold or Eunice.

BILINGUAL EDUCATION The attempt to integrate Spanish-speaking students into the American mainstream as slowly as possible by keeping them fluent in their ancestral tongue.

BILLBOARD An outdoor structure used for commercial purposes, like the Goodyear blimp or a willing Olympic gold medalist.

BIMBO Uncomplimentary appellation for a gaudy young woman with an impressive aptitude for latching onto moneyed men, despite (or perhaps because of) the fact that her combined bust and hip measurements tend to exceed her IQ.

BIODEGRADABLE Desirable to an environmentally aware consumer because of its tendency to decompose, preferably *after* being used.

BIRTHING Giving birth, esp. as practiced by socially correct women who have attended classes on the subject in tandem with their sensitive mates. Gerund form of the verb *to birth,* conjugated in the present indicative as follows:

I birth	we birth
thou birthest	you birth
he she } births it	they birth

BISTRO   A boutique that serves hot meals; notable for charmingly indecipherable handwritten menus that effectively disguise the prices.

BLACK HOLE   A celestial vacuum cleaner.

BLAME   Tossing the hot potato of responsibility to an innocent bystander, usually a male of European ancestry.

BLOCKBUSTER   A movie seen by everyone, mainly because everyone is seeing it. Good news for producers who spend liberally on special effects to win an audience; bad news for modest films that have to resort to shameless gimmicks like poignancy or memorable acting.

B.O.   The natural aroma that spawned an industry, coincidentally not long after the emergence of mass-market advertising.

BOHEMIAN   An urban hipster who rejects mindless bourgeois comforts for the exhilaration of chasing cockroaches around a one-room walk-up.

BOMB   **1.** An explosive device that, when dropped by a plane, can flatten an apartment building. **2.** (chiefly U.S.) An expensive film that, when dropped by the public, can flatten a movie studio and numerous careers. **3.** (chiefly Brit.) A blockbuster.

BOOK REVIEW A brief but informative essay that spares readers the ordeal of digesting an actual book.

BOOKCASE A piece of furniture used in America to display bowling trophies and Elvis collectibles.

BOOKS Nonfattening sandwiches of paper and print, now largely consumed either for information or titillation; in the pre-electronic era, one of the chief sources of private inspiration and civilized pleasure.

BOOM BOX A high-decibel assault weapon carried in the streets and on public conveyances by urban youths, specifically to bedevil older folks whose hearing has remained unimpaired— at least until that moment. No trace has been found of the NYU professor who, on a recent stroll through the South Bronx, retaliated by blasting the neighborhood with Bach's *Concerto in D Minor for Four Harpsichords*.

BORN-AGAIN Describing one who believes he has cast his lot with the elect; a state of grace attained by converts to fundamentalist Christianity, vegetarianism, bodybuilding, Transcendental Meditation, Amway and—for about six months—true love.

BOSS A personal dictator appointed to those of us fortunate enough to live in free societies.

BOUTIQUE A salon consecrated to the merchandising of snobbery and overpriced apparel.

Boxing A mutual infliction of brain damage for the amusement of the public.

Braces A barbed-wire fence erected around a virgin's teeth to snag the tongues of overly ardent suitors.

Brain The seat of cerebration; the source of wonder; a two-room cottage occupied by an artist and an accountant engaged in a perpetual tug-of-war.

Brainwashing See CONSCIOUSNESS-RAISING.

Brassiere The original anti-gravity device.

Broadway Musical Currently a circus without elephants or memorable tunes, aimed at impressionable out-of-towners who mistake garishness for entertainment, and grandiosity for talent.

Bulimia Retched excess.

Bull Market In stock speculation, the triumph of greed over fear.

Ant.: **Bear Market** Fear's revenge.

Bully A belligerent oaf who torments the innocent to enhance his self-esteem; e.g., a gang member, a mobster, a beefy fourth-grader or an influential theater critic.

Bureaucracy A stubborn clog in the sewer pipe of government.

Bureaucrat The mole-like creature who enjoys lifelong job security and a generous pension for making sure the pipe stays clogged.

Burger The ultimate humiliation of a bovine: transformation into an edible cow-patty topped with pickles and ketchup. The bovine's revenge: finding fulfillment as a well-placed clog in a human coronary artery.

BURNOUT   The enervated condition of those who no longer delight in having their blood pressure raised on a daily basis; the misery of Sisyphus after his ten-thousandth roll.

BUSING   Sending delegations of innocent children as sacrificial offerings to the god of race relations.

BUZZWORDS   The verbal equivalent of dressing for success in the business world, where a vocabulary that includes *leveraging* or *incremental* will lift your status as surely as a power suit or corporate suspenders.

CABLE TV A household convenience that multiplies our entertainment options so we can entirely dispense with friends, conversation, reading, our mates and other archaic diversions.

CADAVER A supporting player who ends up on the cutting-room floor. A physician's first patient, and the only one who absolutely cannot die or sue for malpractice. Also the reason most medical students never feel the need to attend horror films.

CAMOUFLAGE A protective mechanism used by the vulnerable to blend in with the background, as with certain insects, military personnel, or white people who use phrases like ''I can dig it'' when addressing an African-American audience.

Campaign   A form of courtship in which rival suitors vie for the hand of a woman who has been wooed, won and abandoned countless times before.

Camping   An overnight excursion that enables nature-starved city-dwellers to commune with the primeval wilderness and its inhabitants, particularly the mosquitoes.

Cancer   A family of insidious wasting diseases caused by virtually everything one eats, breathes or touches in modern industrialized society. Also thought to result from repression of anger, unlike HEART ATTACK (q.v.), which snuffs those who *express* their anger.

Canonization   Posthumous elevation to sainthood; a state of grace attained by religious leaders through miracles, by politicians via assassination, and by rock stars as the result of a timely drug overdose.

Capitalist   A host who orders his guests to prepare a lavish multicourse dinner, then proceeds to devour the largest and choicest portions himself.

Capital Punishment   The controversial right of the state to end a life by gassing, shooting, hanging, needling or quick-frying; believed effective as a deterrent to future crimes by the same individual. The common fate of incorrigible convicts and homeless pets.

CARBON MONOXIDE POISONING   An effective means of suicide, formerly accomplished surreptitiously inside one's garage; now achievable by anyone who inhales deeply in Mexico City.

CAREERISM   The widespread belief that life offers nothing so sublime as the opportunity to climb two or three steps up the corporate pyramid over a period of forty years.

CAR PHONE   The ideal gift for a sadistic boss who tends to lose control when he shouts into the receiver.

CASINO   A gaudy smoke-filled den presided over by men with no necks and patronized by busloads of congenital optimists.

CASTE SYSTEM   A hierarchy of rigid class divisions imported from the Hindus for the purpose of curbing runaway democracy in America. Examples:

salaried workers	doctors	psychiatrists	preppies
hourly workers	nurses	psychologists	horses
	patients	astrologers	everyone else

CATALOGS   Little stores that arrive by mail until we have a shopping mall where our living room used to be.

CAT SHOW   An opportunity for feline fanciers to purr over the latest perversions of selective breeding.

CELEBRITY   A professional famous person; one who, for a few seasons of notoriety and wealth, must endure rabid fans, vicious tabloid reporters and the company of other celebrities.

CELIBACY A respite from the pleasures and perils of sexual congress; a way of life traditionally practiced by Catholic priests, monks, Shakers, stamp collectors, overly zealous careerists, "Star Trek" fans, hermits and amoebas.

CENSORSHIP Use of excessive force by society's thought-police in both lanes of the political highway. On the right: the squelching of provocative art, language, ideas or manners in an attempt to protect the public, which is generally oblivious to the squelchees until the precise moment they are squelched. On the left: the suppression of politically incorrect writers or campus speakers who threaten to expose the dogma *du jour* as so much piffle. In either case: the dream of every struggling troublemaker who aspires to instant fame.

CEO Corporate Ego in Overdrive.

CHAMELEON A small reptile that can change its color to suit its environment. See also YUPPIE.

CHANTEUSE A female cabaret singer whose fame and panache are such that she needn't worry about hitting all the notes.

CHARACTER (archaic) Steadfast personal integrity combined with an unostentatious decency of conduct; now considered maladaptive behavior by influential members of the psychiatric profession.

CHARISMA An electromagnetic force that commonly attracts voters, bedmates, autograph seekers and assassins.

Checkout Counter   A foretaste of hell at the supermarket: a place where one stands immobilized with secret fury while watching the patrons on other, *longer* lines move through the proceedings with supernatural swiftness. See also TOLL-BOOTH.

Chemotherapy   A medical bargain that allows cancer patients to buy some extra time in exchange for their hair and vitality.

Chess   A cerebral wrestling-match in which the object is to pin your opponent's ego to the mat. A slow-motion spectator sport that enables its fans to break for cocktails, enjoy a five-course dinner, and return to the arena without having missed any of the action.

Chewing Gum   Television for the teeth.

Chic   Considered smart without the deadening implication of intelligence.

Childhood   The rapidly shrinking interval between infancy and first arrest on a drug or weapons charge.

Children's Names, Fashionable   The *Jason*ing and *Caitlin*ing of an entire generation by parents of contemporary sensibilities, who seem unconcerned that they might be creating the next century's "Elmer" and "Bertha."

Chocolate   Luscious ripples of fat extracted from a Latin American bean and soon added to our waistlines.

Cholesterol   **1.** (U.S.) The killer sludge; a stealthy assassin waiting for assistance from just one more cheeseburger to close an artery and a life. **2.** (France) The primary ingredient in the longevity-enhancing national diet, traditionally consumed in conjunction with wine and nonchalance.

CHRISTMAS A warm and cheery two-month festival that celebrates the joy of retail merchandise.

CHRISTMAS CARDS An annual opportunity to discover who your friends are, esp. by holding out until the final week and scratching the delinquent names from your list. Another effective technique is to snub marginal friends who snubbed you the year before, which virtually assures that they will send you a card; one may thus sustain a satisfying lifelong pattern of alternate-year snubbing.

CHUTZPAH The endearing effrontery of a mugger who threatens to sue his victim for bleeding all over his new suit.

CIGARETTE A flimsy paper cylinder packed with dried leaves and set afire for the purpose of inhaling the smoke and toxic substances produced therefrom. An indispensable prop, throughout most of the twentieth century, for tough-talking adults and aspirants to that status.

CINEMA Pretentious label for movies in general, and for pretentious movies in particular.

CLASS (archaic) A gently noble demeanor that used to be associated with good breeding but now invites a steady stream of wisecracks on TV sitcoms.

CLASS REUNION A periodic gathering of elderly adolescents, promising a wistful glimpse of our first love, an opportunity to resurrect ancient banter with old cronies, and the joy of discovering who has failed more miserably or aged more absurdly than we have.

CLASSICAL MUSIC (archaic) Celestial vibrations from the human soul, notable in our era for being nonexistent for the first time since the late Middle Ages. Evidence that such music once existed still may be discovered in an occasional record store, usually in a single bin sequestered somewhere in a back aisle next to the polka and bouzouki albums.

CLERGYMAN The official custodian of a religious congregation's ancient tribal beliefs, appointed so that the members can leave spiritual matters to a qualified professional while they go about the business of sinning and making a living.

CLIQUE A group of insiders who greet outsiders with their backsides; a closed circle of asses.

CLONE Identical offspring produced by means of asexual reproduction; explains the proliferation of fast-food restaurants, tract homes and local TV news anchors on the American scene.

CLUB 1. In current parlance, a dark den to which young people repair under cover of night, where they gyrate to state-of-the-art music, display their state-of-the-art hairdos and affect a carefully practiced state-of-the-art attitude that will endear them to their peers. 2. In high schools of yore, an association of students with a common interest in minerals or philately.

COAL MINER A heroic laboring man who toils a lifetime in Hades and risks an early demise so that his children might do the same.

Coast, The Where creative types sell their souls for a beach house with a Jacuzzi, unlike their eastern compatriots, who are known to sell theirs for a good table at Elaine's.

Cocaine The recreational drug of choice for the Smart Young People of the post-Vietnam era, who found it daring and glamorous to sniff the residue from the pulverized leaves of a Bolivian shrub.

Cockroach An ugly, greasy, universally reviled six-legged freeloader with a fondness for procreation and leftovers. One of nature's all-time success stories, suggesting that the gods love an obscene joke.

Cocktail Party How middle-class achievers socialize with their comrades: standing face-to-face while wielding small, hollow shields that may be refilled on a regular basis.

Cocooning A college-educated Baby Boomer's idea of heaven: curling up on the sofa with a just-opened bag of munchies, a cat purring nearby and, on TV, a 72-hour "Three Stooges" marathon.

Codependency A fashionable malady concocted by self-help gurus so that mentally healthy women might have a psychological disorder to call their own.

Coffee A mud-brown beverage consisting of granulated tropical beans methodically dribbled into scalding water, and consumed in copious quantities for its power to produce a satisfactory level of nervous agitation.

COHABITATION Living together with probable intent to practice conjugation; a semi-scandalous lifestyle shared by young libertines and elderly pensioners, although not usually in the same dwelling quarters.

COLA Brown champagne; an effervescent, sugar-saturated, heavily promoted libation made from an obscure species of African nut and occasionally enhanced with extract from the leaves of a popular South American shrub. (See COCAINE.) Ranks among the world's most beloved beverages, despite its nondescript flavor and the apparent narrowness of its age appeal: on TV ads nobody who drinks it appears to be younger than seventeen or older than nineteen. Medical studies have yet to determine if the brew possesses rejuvenating powers or whether heavy users should be advised to make out their wills during spring break.

COLLECTIBLE An addictive substance that demands a staggering portion of our discretionary income, so that we might die with a complete set of vintage Pez dispensers and $180 in the bank.

COLLEGE 1. (archaic) A fabled oasis consecrated to higher learning and inspired mischief; a realm of giddy camaraderie . . . of late-night debates on politics, pizza toppings or Plato's Theory of Forms . . . of brisk walks and exhilarating talks on frosty quadrangles . . . of ancient cupolas and gothic towers aglow in the fading winter light, as one's youthful heart quickens with romantic hopes and merriment. 2. A politically correct establishment that indoctrinates contemporary students with economically correct money-making skills while it introduces their parents to the concept of poverty.

COLLEGE ATHLETES **1.** (football and basketball only) Burly Cinderellas whisked out of the ghetto to lead a life of unimagined luxury and privilege in the public arena, then shuttled home in rags at the end of four years. Sometimes the prince comes calling with a professional contract; more often it's just the local drug dealer. **2.** (all other sports) Actual college students who may still be recruited to fill the rosters of the fencing and badminton teams and the like, since nobody will be watching anyway.

COLLEGE BOARD SCORES The standardized rating we foolishly thought would determine the quality of our future. In later life, one of few remaining scraps of evidence intelligent washouts can use to compare themselves favorably with the corporate jocks who invariably leapfrog over them.

COMIC BOOKS Literature for the semiliterate; art for the artless; frozen Saturday-morning television. A bonanza for anyone who saves the premiere issue of *Crabman* or *The Avenging Mollusk*.

COMMERCIALS Maddeningly memorable messages occasionally interrupted by several minutes of forgettable programming.

COMMITMENT Surrendering our personal freedom so that we might enter a long-term relationship or a mental ward. The latter option at least promises peaceful afternoons in the company of our peers, coloring with crayons or rolling little sausages out of clay.

COMMITTEE   A grotesque creature with multiple heads and twice as many feet, no three of them pointing in the same direction.

COMMUNISM   Liberation of the people from the burdens of liberty. A twentieth-century epidemic that killed off the healthy opposition and kept the remaining comrades in a comatose state for generations, although a few of them were revived sufficiently every four years to win the Olympics.

COMMUNITY COLLEGE   An institution of useful learning whose undergraduate student body resembles that of the local high school with both ends of the bell curve lopped off.

COMMUTERS   Dedicated masochists who venture miles out of their way to find trouble.

COMPETITION   The timeless struggle to secure a favorable niche in the presence of one's rivals, as practiced by walruses that lock tusks over a harem of walrettes, or the twenty-seven brands of tortilla chip that commit mayhem for a place on our pantry shelf.

COMPUTER   A nimble electronic brain devoid of animal passions and human wit, and therefore admirably suited to the contemporary corporate environment.

COMPUTER LITERACY   Ability to move words on a screen without ever appreciating their capacity to move minds.

CONCERT   Onstage talent playing to a chorus of coughs.

CONDOM   An object similar in appearance to a balloon, although it is rarely inflated with helium or tied into funny animal shapes at children's birthday parties.

CONDOMINIUM   A private residential unit that re-creates the ambience of suburban tract housing without the nuisance of private lawns and gardens; a domicile favored especially by young professionals and retired folks, who apparently don't mind paying substantial monthly fees on property they already own.

CONFORMITY   Fear of being publicly identified as an individual, different from and therefore inferior to the norm; accounts for the open-fronted uniform worn virtually unchanged by corporate males for half a century.

CONNOISSEUR   One who attains an obsessive knowledge of wines, audio equipment, cats or French cheeses so as to confer a sense of inadequacy on those who would simply enjoy them.

CONSCIOUSNESS-RAISING   The fine art of teaching well-adjusted citizens to view themselves as victims of oppression.

CONSERVATION   The subversive notion that a tract of unspoiled rain forest, for example, might be more valuable than the fast-food hamburgers that can be produced on its ruins.

CONSERVATIVE   In the U.S., a decent fellow who counsels the poor to earn pennies for their daily bread, while he and his family dine nightly on filet mignon. In the former Soviet Union, a Communist.

CONSPICUOUS CONSUMPTION   The tendency of the newly rich to convert income into material trappings of a vulgar and ostentatious nature, thereby earning the scorn of their betters, the envy of their peers and the wrath of the less fortunate.

Conspiracy An intricate plot that, when described by its victim, generally results in confinement to a padded cell, but when fabricated by authors or film directors, usually earns them a new hacienda in the hills.

Consultant A jobless person who shows executives how to work.

Consumer One who delights advertisers by acquiring unnecessary products in accordance with the motto ''I spend, therefore I am.''

Contact Lenses Elf-sized eyewear notable for providing the benefits of glasses without the unsightly frames, and for sharpening one's powers of detection when dropped onto a high-pile carpet or lush green lawn.

Contraceptive A pill or gizmo that enables a couple to savor the mirth without the birth.

Convenience Store A profitable mini-market, so named because it conveniently spares armed robbers the trouble of engineering a heist at the local bank.

Converts Gullible folks who have agreed to let an outside contractor renovate their souls.

Cool Sufficiently smug, careless and inarticulate to gain leadership status in adolescent society.

Coping Late twentieth-century substitute for living. An abnormal tolerance for the intolerable.

CORPORATE CULTURE The group mentality to which a company hireling must conform or die; not, as one might expect, a reference to in-house drama workshops, chamber ensembles or Great Books discussion groups. One of the supreme oxymorons of our time.

CORPORATION A miniature totalitarian state governed by a hierarchy of unelected officials who take a dim view of individualism, free speech, equality and eggheads. The backbone of all Western democracies.

CORRECTIONAL FACILITY Rent-free public housing for thieves, rapists, muggers, murderers, deadbeats, extortionists, drug fiends and other assorted malcontents who are thought to benefit from confinement in each other's company.

COSMETICS An arsenal of facial enhancements commonly applied in excess by women and male celebrities who feel the need to look embalmed.

COST-EFFECTIVE The only type of activity that would be worth pursuing if accountants ruled the world, which of course they do.

COUNTRY AND WESTERN MUSIC **1.** (archaic) A twanging harmonic concoction, American as hominy grits, that once chronicled the simple bovine joys and miseries of wayward Baptists, cowboys and truck drivers; much beloved in the lands beyond the urban fringe, wherever the corn grew high and honest folks ate pork barbecue; redolent of summer nights on the road, fifty miles from the nearest honky-tonk and even farther from home.

2. Slick pop tunes currently produced by marketing experts for a mass audience of redneck wannabes.

COUNTRY CLUB An enclosed oasis where, with a little influence and a substantial cash outlay, one may qualify to hit golf balls in the presence of local white community leaders and their spouses.

COUPLE The basic unit of social validity at restaurants, country inns, the theater and other pleasant destinations; solitary folks unwilling to break the unspoken taboo may still find a warm welcome at psychiatrists' offices and funeral homes.

CPR An emergency exercise that helps concerned onlookers feel useful while the victim expires.

CRACK Kiddie cocaine; a potentially lethal substance peddled by juvenile street tycoons to their restless peers, who find themselves overwhelmed by a life of compulsory education and Saturday-morning television.

CRAFTSPERSON A liberal arts graduate gone to pasture, esp. after a nerve-jangling tussle with the business world. A placid soul who seeks a life-enhancing alternative to sweating over contracts and deadlines, then finds it by creating ceramic vegetables or gingham bunnies.

CREATIVITY Currently a code word for *self-expression,* which itself is a code word for *self-indulgence.*

CREDIT CARD Plastic passport to the valley of the shadow of debt.

CREDIT RATING A confidential report card circulated among creditors for the purpose of ascertaining whether a given consumer has incurred enough debts to be considered a sound risk.

CREMATION The fairly common practice of flame-broiling the deceased; a dose of hellfire with or without damnation.

CRITIC, LITERARY A solemn interpreter who listens to the ravings of modern poets and *fictionmeisters,* then pretends to translate them for a skeptical public. One who rhapsodizes over the most perversely obscure works because they make his job *necessary*.

CRITIC, THEATER A skulking submarine that can sink an entire production with one well-aimed torpedo.

CRITICAL Acutely diseased, acutely displeased or, in the case of those who remain conscious while being moved to the mortician's on-deck circle, both diseased *and* displeased.

CRUISE 1. *n* An opportunity for middle-class voyagers to consume mass quantities of food and drink, pursue short-term romance, vomit periodically and take snapshots of an island or port between meals. 2. *vb* To pursue short-term romance without the aid of a boat.

CRYONICS The gentle art of freezing corpses, or parts thereof, in hope of resurrecting them as future dinner guests or talking heads.

CUDDLING A sweetly chaste form of intimacy that tends to make the average man feel like a muzzled hound on a fox hunt.

CULT An in-crowd that accepts misfits on the condition that they surrender their souls and occasionally their lives; most inductees join without hesitation.

CULT FILM A movie seen about fifty times by about that many people.

CULTURE The visible evidence of a tribe of bacteria, as observed by microbiologists or cynics.

CULTURE SHOCK A form of stress precipitated by sudden exposure to strange new manners and mores; a temporary befuddlement experienced by Americans when they travel abroad, and even more so when they return home.

CURRICULUM A harness devised by educational bureaucrats to turn thoroughbred teachers into cart horses.

CYBERPUNK The futuristic bandit of the information highway: a black-hatted gunslinger with a microchip on his shoulder and a modem in his holster. A high-tech juvenile delinquent who lives for the joy of raiding establishment data bases, and whose emerging subculture combines the warmth of computer technology with the lyricism of punk rock.

CYNIC An idealist whose rose-colored glasses have been removed, snapped in two and stomped into the ground, immediately improving his vision.

DATE RAPE Unilateral escalation of a courtship to its inevitable conclusion, without the usual niceties of flowers and consent. Also, what a contemporary college student is likely to be charged with if he forgets to say, "May I?"

DATING An elaborate prelude to mating that fulfills much the same function as the sniffing ritual in dogs, but without its forthright honesty.

DECADENCE Civilization in its overripe phase: soft, pulpy, sensuous, and likely to turn to mush when sufficient pressure is applied.

DECONSTRUCTIONISM The theory that one's personal response to a work of literature is more important than the work itself; not surprisingly a popular doctrine among creatively impaired English professors, who can now rank their efforts above those of Shakespeare and Dickens.

DEFENSE INDUSTRY A loose association of hardware companies, any of which might be recommended as a sound investment whenever large numbers of living people are officially designated as targets.

DEMAGOGUE Traditionally a politician skilled in the use of incendiary rhetoric to inflame a mob. Now more likely to be a talk-show personality whose utterances consist entirely of calculated applause lines.

DEMOGRAPHICS A portrait of an audience painted by statisticians and composed entirely of numbers; a work of art prized in the marketplace as long as it depicts a college-educated, free-spending twenty-five-to-forty-four-year-old manager/professional with at least twice the household income of Joe Average. Whether the portrait reveals any emotional depth or subtlety is beside the point.

DENIAL How an optimist keeps from becoming a pessimist.

DENTIST An amiable health professional who, following the devastating insult of rejection from medical school, must endure a lifetime of Dr. Mengele analogies, the aroma of decaying tooth pulp, and possibly the worst scenery this side of a proctologist's office.

DENTURES   Two rows of artificial ivories that may be removed periodically to frighten one's grandchildren or provide accompaniment to Spanish music.

DEPRESSION   An affliction of individuals or economies that have tumbled into a well with ice-coated walls; if no help arrives, one has little choice but to keep amused and wait for a thaw.

DESIGNER LABEL   A minuscule patch of material that, whether concealed or in open view, automatically doubles the price of any object it adorns. Once confined to original garments in exclusive cosmopolitan boutiques; now likely to be seen on everything from sweatsuits to prosthetic kneecaps.

DEVELOPER   A magician who commands shopping malls and office parks to appear on the ruins of historic sites, family farms, woodlands and widows' homes.

DICTATOR   The alpha male in a tribe of baboons.

DIET   The temporary triumph of will over metabolism.

DIFFERENTLY ABLED   Abled apart from the norm; enjoying an unusual level of ableness, so to speak. The preferred, socially correct euphemism (as of this writing) for *handicapped,* which in its day was a passable euphemism for the needlessly honest *crippled.*

DINNER THEATER   An establishment that cleverly escapes judgment on the quality of its food by distracting its patrons with a lively show, and likewise eludes criticism of its entertainment by keeping the jaws of the audience continuously occupied with more substantial fare.

DINOSAURS   **1.** A clan of awesome Mesozoic beasts now thought to be the ancestors of the chicken. **2.** Any other oversized, ill-adapted creatures doomed to eventual extinction; e.g., dirigibles, ocean liners, the Soviet Union or major TV networks.

DIRECTIONS   How to get from Point A to Point B, preferably without encountering Points C, K or Q along the way. Something a real man never asks for when lost on the open road, at least in the presence of a female passenger; instead, he deploys his gender-based internal compass, comments on the rustic beauty of the scenic route and prays for a familiar landmark.

DISADVANTAGED   Denied the privilege (according to white middle-class sociologists) of having been born to white middle-class parents.

DISCO   The thumping mutant offspring of rock music, electronically engineered until all vestiges of humanity have been successfully extirpated. Flourished in the late 1970s, esp. among trendy urbanites, who would trail clouds of white powder as they lined up at clubs with entrance standards to rival those of MIT.

DISPOSABLE   Designed to be used briefly and tossed away forever, like razors, paper plates, income or friends.

DISSERTATION An interminable collection of footnotes strung together by an impossibly tedious narrative; the obligatory price of admission to the grazing pastures of academe.

DIVORCE Termination of a marriage before either spouse can terminate the other. According to custom, both parties enter into a knockdown legal battle that is always won by their attorneys and usually lost by their children.

DNA A complex organic molecule characterized as the building block of life and appropriately shaped like a spiral staircase to nowhere.

DO-IT-YOURSELF Hire-a-professional-one-month-later-to-redo-it-for-$800-more-than-it-would-have-cost-originally.

DOG FOOD The main course for man's best friend and senior citizens on fixed incomes.

DONATION Money given voluntarily to a charity or demanded in specific amounts by museums too high-minded to charge admission.

DOWNSIZING Corporate euphemism for "Let's save a little money by firing half our staff and making the other suckers work twice as hard."

DOWNWARD MOBILITY The decline and fall of the middle-class liberal arts graduate, casualty of a tight economy and perhaps an innate disinclination for business; a gradual estrangement from bourgeois respectability and the company of moneyed friends, which the wise may secretly regard as a liberation.

DRAG QUEEN   A man impersonating the kind of woman who always did remind you of a man impersonating a woman.

DYSFUNCTIONAL FAMILY   A term used by psychologists to describe any household occupied by two or more related individuals.

Ecosystem The environment viewed as a delicately balanced Rube Goldberg contraption: discarded Balloon (A) chokes Duck (B), which expires and pollutes Pond (C), which kills Minnow (D), which drives away Pied-billed Grebe (E), which distresses Birdwatcher (F), who contributes to Friends of Wetlands (G), which lobbies in Congress (H), which passes Antipollution Law (I), which cuts profits at Toxico, Inc. (J), which lays off 20 percent of its Payroll (K) including Stanley Frimko (L), who now has more time to walk in the park with his daughter Danielle (M), who lets go of Balloon (N), which unfortunately pops in the Stratosphere (O) and drops into Pond (P), where it catches the attention of Duck (Q).

EDITOR   In the publishing industry, a diligent intellectual drudge condemned to a lifetime of embarrassingly meager pay, so that multimillion-dollar contracts might be awarded to semiliterate celebrities for their ghostwritten memoirs.

EGO   A helium-filled balloon that often lifts the ambitious to lofty destinations, where the change in pressure can cause it to pop unexpectedly. More practical citizens inflate their balloons with their own breath, taking care to avoid the pins and needles of ill-intentioned colleagues. The most sensible of all carry an uninflated balloon in their back pocket for safekeeping.

ELDER STATESMAN   A political reprobate whose sins are forgiven as he begins to resemble our grandparents.

ELECTRIC GUITAR   A rigid musical appendage worn below the belt by the high priests of rock, who then commence to strum it before a delirious congregation.

ELEVATOR   A tiny room that ascends or descends at the whim of its occupants, who listen in rapt silence as pleasantly embalmed pop tunes anesthetize their souls.

EMBALMING   The metamorphosis of the deceased into a waxwork bearing a superficial resemblance to the living person, who is no longer around for comparison.

ENDANGERED SPECIES   Any biological tribe whose chances of survival are impaired by wanton persecution, withering competition, maladaptive behavior or the destruction of a congenial environment; e.g., mountain gorillas, humpback whales, giant anteaters and teachers of Classical Greek.

ENDORPHINS An indwelling pleasure drug triggered by activities that satisfy our individual needs; e.g., when a jogger jogs, a rock climber climbs or a serial killer finds a fresh neck in a dark alley.

ENDORSEMENT The common practice, esp. among celebrities, of renting out one's good name to promote a denture cream or a politician—whichever represents the better career move.

ENTERTAINERS Heirs to the wandering bards and jugglers who used to earn their bread by amusing the king; today they travel in limousines and phone their business managers about buying the castle.

ENTERTAINMENT INDUSTRY A vast network of business empires whose role is to divert us as society crumbles, and to accelerate the crumbling so that we require more diversion. Comparable to the band that played aboard the *Titanic,* except that in this case they've also supplied the iceberg.

ENTREPRENEUR A professional opportunist; one who satisfies his own material cravings by catering to those of the public.

ENVELOPE, PUSHING THE A slow, deliberate and continuous erosion of genteel media taboos, with no end in sight: a mild expletive here, an exposed buttock there . . . then a harsher expletive and *two* exposed buttocks, not necessarily from the same individual . . . then images of bare-buttocked teenagers using expletives in the presence of nuns . . . nuns in their *underwear . . . naked* nuns . . . naked *dead* nuns decapitated on live TV . . . as we sit on our sofas and pass the nachos.

Erogenous Zone By current reckoning, any region of the human topography with the possible exception of the elbows.

Erudite Exhibiting a degree of book learning fatal to success in any business or romantic enterprise.

ESP The unexplained power of certain finely tuned individuals to receive radio signals from beyond the usual broadcasting range, often including *tomorrow's* programs; unfortunately they never seem to catch the racing results or the stock market reports.

Espresso Eurocoffee; a dense brown beverage served in dollhouse cups to fashionable weekend bohemians.

Establishment The legitimate mafia that runs any society; where radical souls go when they die or receive an offer too good to refuse.

Ethics An unspoken code of decency that once governed most business and professional transactions, at least theoretically; now a fluctuating commodity that declines in direct proportion to the amount of money at stake.

Ethnic Group An extended family that bickers with its neighbors and occasionally invades their turf to shed a little neighborly blood; not to be confused with STREET GANG. In multinational societies that encourage cross-breeding, the old ethnic groups are giving way to newer, more cohesive (and even more identifiable) ones; e.g., feminists, fundamentalists, gays, vegetarians, yuppies, academics, metalheads, Knights of Columbus, direct-marketing professionals, witches, bikers, bodybuilders, Rotarians, rock climbers, New Agers, Elks, Mormons, mathematicians and the U.S. Marines. Of all the aforementioned groups, only the vegetarians and the yuppies have established their own distinctive cuisines.

ETHNIC JOKE A vaguely conspiratorial method of communicating unpalatable truths and half-truths about various minority groups, esp. those presumed not to be present in the audience.

ETIQUETTE A system of ritualized courtesies, most of which concern proper use of the fork; a social code devised and memorized by members of the upper classes for the purpose of screening out raffish pretenders to their ranks.

EULOGY A glowing account of the deceased, generally delivered by a clergyman who must glance at the page to get the name right. Often the first kind words ever said about the subject of the oration, occasionally embroidered with wishful inaccuracies, and always too late to be savored by the one in the box.

EUPHEMISM The bland artificial coating on a bitter pill; e.g., ''The Cuthbertson appendectomy terminated in a *negative patient health-care outcome.*''

EUTHANASIA Generally more proficient at math and science than euthanamerica.

Evil Archaic judgmental term formerly used to insult the ethically disadvantaged and the morally challenged.

Evolution A biological relay race hurtling onward and occasionally upward from the ancient muck, as *trilobites* and *pterodactyls* pass the baton to aardvarks and claims adjusters.

Executive One who executes middle managers, esp. while wearing an expensive suit.

Exhaustion Sufficient cause for the hospitalization of a celebrity; the normal state of existence for the rest of the working world.

Exhibitionist A naked man commonly arrested for standing in a window so that he might be glimpsed by a woman standing outside; when a naked *woman* is in the window and the man is standing outside, he is then arrested as a Peeping Tom.

Exhumation Disturbing the beauty sleep of an old rotter.

Existentialism A French school of philosophy popular for a time during the 1950s and 1960s; taught its adherents how to wear a black turtleneck, dangle a cigarette from the lips and strike just the correct pose of dour worldliness—all useful tools for seducing female graduate students over coffee.

Exorcism Expulsion of the vile demons that hold us in thrall, generally accomplished through medieval rituals and, on rare occasions, psychoanalysis.

Expatriate The probable status of this lexicographer following the probable reception of this dictionary.

Experience In the working world, something you can't get unless you've already got it, in which case you probably don't want any more of it.

EXPERIMENT The fine art of fudging scientific data so that they mesh with one's original hypothesis.

EXPERTS Heavily credentialed wisefolk whose advice carries the stamp of unassailable authority, like the nutritionists of our youth who told us to gorge ourselves on whole milk and red meat.

EXPLOITATION Subjugation of the desperate by the overly energetic.

EXTINCTION The end of the line for creatures that cannot or *will* not adapt to an increasingly hostile environment, which is why the future belongs to cockroaches and M.B.A.'s.

EXTORTION The forced surrender of one's lunch money as a tolerable alternative to something even less pleasant: a thrashing by the schoolyard bully, a one-way car ride with the mob or an audit by the Internal Revenue Service.

Face-lift Temporary restoration of the visage we wore in youth, but one size smaller.

Factionalism The abiding human need to create group conflicts based on religion, politics, race, gender, class or whether toilet paper should be pulled over or under the roll.

Fad A folly committed by enough of the right people to confer upon it the badge of status.

Fans Modern descendants of the Dionysiacs of ancient Greece, who would customarily devour the object of their worship.

Farmer **1.** CEO of an efficient multimillion-dollar business that manufactures chemically enhanced animal and vegetable products for nationwide consumption. **2.** (archaic) A sturdy yeoman who sweated over the soil, took pride in his labor, fed the good people of his county, and produced an unbroken chain of descendants to inherit his humble patch of earth—until one of them sold out to a condo developer and absconded with the loot.

Fascism Nationalism with obsessive-compulsive tendencies.

Fashion Today's rage, tomorrow's chuckle.

Fast-food Restaurants Tidy, congenial roadside bistros that clog the nation's highways and the arteries of their patrons.

Fast Track Evidence that corporations help those whom God would help anyway.

Fax A modern enhancement of the telephone, enabling us to send and receive illegible information in seconds; also ideal for communicating bad news without the inconvenience of having to talk to the person at the other end.

Federal Budget A miraculous machine that continually cranks out more money than it takes in; unfortunately not yet licensed for use in the home.

Federal Deficit The bill for operating the aforesaid machine.

Feminist A woman who intends to fulfill her destiny by aping the worst traits of her oppressors. Also a man who believes that siding with women will get him more dates.

FERN BAR   A genteel drinking establishment catering to upscale urban women and their mild-mannered consorts; any tavern that serves frozen kiwi-flavored drinks in a palm-court setting.

FIBER   Edible wood-pulp said to aid digestion and prolong life, so that we might enjoy an extra eight or ten years in which to consume wood-pulp.

FICTION   The fine art of narrative literary invention; notable at present for meticulously re-creating the mindless monotony of contemporary life for the entertainment of English professors and their captive students.

FILMMAKER   Fabricator of celluloid entertainments, esp. those the major studios refuse to produce. Usurper, in postliterate society, of the cultural throne once graced by poets and authors.

FINAL EXAMS   A series of Judgment Days endured by students throughout their academic careers and often for many years thereafter, shortly before they wake up in a cold sweat.

FIREARMS   Lethal weapons that all Americans are constitutionally entitled to keep in their homes, where they tend to be used less to ward off intruders than to settle family disputes in a decisive and permanent manner.

FISHING   A venerable contest in which modern man pits his intelligence and technology against the native wit of primitive aquatic vertebrates, and generally finishes second.

Fitness Salvation through perspiration; an unfair physical advantage in the struggle for survival, which of course *should* be determined on the basis of character, congeniality, and an appreciation of eighteenth-century English prose.

Folk Singers Shaggy bards who emerge from underground during times of social unrest, let out a few nasal roars, then return to coffee-house hibernation until the next major upheaval.

Food chain The vast hierarchy of predators, with plankton at the bottom and marketing executives at the top.

Formula A precise recipe concocted by pediatricians as a substitute for mother's milk, or by hack writers as a ticket to best-sellerdom.

Foundation Grant Bourgeois beneficence that enables unmarketable artists to continue expressing their contempt for bourgeois values.

Fraternity A secret society for the indoctrination of college boys into the time-honored male traditions of drinking, debauchery, backslapping and barfing.

Free Gift The kind you receive when you pay for a mail-order offer, as opposed to the kind that costs you nothing.

Freedom of Religion The constitutionally guaranteed right to worship one's God anywhere except on public property, which today must be made safe for school-sponsored rap concerts and alternative-lifestyles discussion groups.

Freedom of Speech The inalienable right of all Americans to have their opinions shouted down by the self-appointed guardians of political correctness.

FREEWAY A clogged artery that connects suburbia with the real world, enabling its mild-mannered residents to shout invigorating oaths, use colorful hand gestures and run their neighbors off the road in preparation for another day at the office.

FUNDAMENTALIST Anyone who takes the Word of God too seriously.

FUNERAL HOME A stately manse occupied by transients who continually receive visitors but lack the energy and inclination to entertain them.

FUR COAT A collection of disemboweled mammal corpses draped around the shoulders of wealthy women and frequently splattered by angry activists in leather sandals.

GAMBLING Risking one's own money for the chance to swipe even more of it from others; e.g., playing at the roulette wheel, betting on horses, buying insurance or putting oneself through law school.

GAME SHOW How television sends us the message that greed is cute.

GARAGE SALE A modest suburban flea market for the unloading of black-velvet paintings, surplus fondue sets, volumes of condensed 1950s best-sellers and other household artifacts that never quite attained the status of heirlooms, except that future owners will be handing them down from sale to sale.

GARBAGE MAN What our parents and teachers warned us we might become if we didn't apply ourselves in school; those diligent scholars who today earn publishing or newspaper salaries might find themselves wishing they had played hooky more often.

GAY (archaic) Festive, lighthearted, free to romp and play; a sunny word appropriated for other uses as the modern world gave us limited occasion to employ it in its original sense.

GAY-BASHING Violence against men who love men by men who fear they love men.

GENES The hand we are dealt in the poker game of life.

GENETIC ENGINEERING Tampering with chromosomes so that science might develop a new miracle cure or a rabbit that plays the banjo.

GENOCIDE How a mad landlord eliminates the family upstairs when evicting them proves to be too much of an ordeal.

GENTLEMAN (archaic) Formerly the male exemplar of honor, nobility and other behavioral relics from the Age of Chivalry; now dismissed as someone with a testosterone deficiency.

GENTRIFICATION The deliberate transformation of a dull or seedy neighborhood into a pretentious one, so as to attract a better class of pedestrian.

GHETTO An isolated enclave populated by kindred types who would be made to feel unwelcome outside its boundaries; e.g., blacks in 1920s Harlem, Jews in 1930s Warsaw, women in secretarial pools, or a class of honor students at an urban high school.

GIFTED CHILDREN   Unfortunate tykes who lack the good sense to hide their talents from overly ambitious parents.

GLIBNESS   The uncanny ability of certain higher primates to issue a steady stream of words without the aid of conscious thought; considered an essential skill among political candidates and other comedians.

GOD   Founder, chairman and CEO of the universe: an invisible boss who readily promotes His more aggressive underlings but has the infinite wisdom to keep them unhappy; neither has He demonstrated undue sympathy toward the meek and the infirm. Has maintained a low profile in recent centuries, apparently preferring to delegate moral authority to military panjandrums, belligerent backwoods preachers, blow-dried TV personalities, politically correct faculty members and other assorted upstarts. The supreme mystery of the ages.

GOLDEN OLDIES   Rock music of ancient vintage (aged at least five years), resurrected from the dead and no longer seeming quite so hideous when compared with the current offerings.

GOLDEN PARACHUTE   A lump-sum fortune awarded to a fired corporate chieftain, presumably because his departure causes company profits to take a sharp upward turn.

GOLF   The art of driving hard, avoiding the rough, surmounting traps and hazards, aiming straight, and arriving on the green at last, only to end up in a hole in the ground before your companions. The favored pastime of businessmen and their cronies, probably without a full appreciation of its metaphorical implications.

GORE   The spilled contents of a broken human body; always a showstopper at the movies and the cause of massive traffic tie-ups at accident sites as inquisitive motorists crane their necks for the possibility of a free glimpse.

GOSSIP   Water-cooler journalism.

GOURMET   A food fetishist; one for whom the correct preparation and consumption of a cheese soufflé has assumed the combined importance of art, science, and Holy Communion.

GRADUATE STUDENT   A newborn intellect that returns to the womb for further incubation, sometimes indefinitely.

GRAFFITI   Urban scrawl; the rude calligraphy of the streets, apt to embellish any wall, statue, subway car or wino within reach of a spray can. Reassuring evidence that today's youth retain a passing acquaintance with the written word.

GREASERS   (archaic) Slick-haired teenage *boulevardiers* whose genially barbaric souls found perfect expression in chrome-encrusted Chevys and doo-wop music. Flourished as a distinct subspecies c. 1954–1966, after which date the hair of adolescent males rapidly migrated south.

GREATNESS   (archaic) Traditionally the highest calling of a restless ego; an inner fire that would burn brilliantly in the service of humanity. What formerly expressed itself through art or statesmanship now finds fulfillment by producing dog-food commercials or masterminding hostile corporate takeovers.

GREED Stuffing a dozen assorted chocolates into one's mouth simultaneously, in the presence of a diabetic.

GREENHOUSE EFFECT A purported global warming that threatens to melt the polar icecaps, flood all cities at sea level and turn the state of New Jersey into a tropical resort.

GROUPIES The self-abasing attendants of a more powerful personage, like the concubines of a rock star or the campaign staff of a rising politician.

GROUP THERAPY A drama-in-the-round staged for the entertainment of a professional therapist, who commands the players to put on a new show each week and charges them for the privilege.

GUERRILLA WARFARE A rude modern mode of back-country combat that preserves all the traditional miseries of war (e.g., serious injury, death, destruction of property) with none of the benefits (glory, decisive victories, spiffy uniforms).

GUILT The uninvited creature perched on our shoulder, chiding us in an uncanny impression of our mother's voice; a sharp remorse that plagues conscientious citizens after a breach of morality or diet, permitting only the scoundrels and skinny folks to forge ahead with their accustomed glee.

Gun Control   An ongoing public debate that might easily be resolved if we allowed everyone to obtain firearms but suspended the production of bullets.

Guru   A self-proclaimed wise man and baby-sitter for the lost children of affluent families; one whose perpetual smile betokens a private joy in fuzzy thinking, freedom from work, and the attentions of nubile waifs.

Hacker A dedicated young computer nerd, frequently mischievous but fundamentally harmless, who spends entire nights clacking away at the keyboard with only a bag of corn chips for companionship. Ranks with gremlins and leprechauns on the Societal Menace Index, while the CYBERPUNK (q.v.) rates a place alongside investment bankers and Attila the Hun.

HAIR The primary medium of self-expression for young folks who have little else to express, and who generally choose to express it in the manner approved by their peer group. Also said to be a status indicator among the white women of Texas, with the honors going to those whose bouffants most nearly approach their total body mass.

HALF-LIFE The span of time required for a thing to deteriorate to 50 percent of its original potency: about twenty-four thousand years for plutonium atoms . . . a few centuries for great civilizations . . . three weeks for a hit song . . . four days for your child's enthusiasm over a new ninety-dollar toy . . . twenty-four hours for the fresh sense of purpose acquired at a motivational seminar . . . fifteen minutes for the warming afterglow of a "feel-good" movie . . . ten seconds for a sudden impulse to shove the papers off your desk, slug the boss and board the next plane to Tahiti.

HANDGUN An indispensable fashion accessory among big-city schoolboys.

HARVARD ACCENT An amusing speech impediment traditionally acquired by students at the nation's most venerated institution of higher learning.

HEALTH A delicate equilibrium that may be upset by smoking too many cigarettes or reading too many alarming medical studies.

HEALTH CLUB A modern temple attended by those who worship the pumped-up trinity of abs, pecs and biceps.

HEALTH FOOD A family of bland, marginally edible grains, beans, sprouts and other vegetative matter that presumably fortifies the body as effectively as it wilts the spirit.

HEALTH INSURANCE Partial protection from the financial ruin that awaits anyone unlucky enough to wake up in an American hospital bed, which is like being partially saved from drowning; currently available to all citizens except those who need it most desperately.

HEART ATTACK A painful modern medical disorder, commonly accompanied by death, that is known to afflict middle-aged men who strive valiantly and hopelessly against their natures, toward goals that make them sick.

HEAVY METAL Amplified noise for teenage boys who feel they must dabble in the Satanic to get a date on Saturday night.

HEDONISM Addiction to a merciless drug called *pleasure,* which is frequently mistaken for happiness. Future slaves may be fatally hooked by a scented bubble bath or by a reckless ride in a Pontiac with a sunroof. In the terminal stages they may be seen to dive out of small airplanes, sail off cliffs or jump from bridges while attached to long rubber umbilical cords, as the addict demands ever-higher doses just to attain the pleasure level of a frog catching a gnat with its tongue.

HEIR The idle offspring of a workaholic.

HERD A cohesive gathering of undifferentiated individuals, as may be observed on the African savannah or at corporate sales conferences. Tradition assigns a different name to each group according to species, e.g.:

a pride of lions
a babble of sportscasters
a yawn of insurance salesmen
a shrill of feminists
a casket of morticians
a smirk of stand-up comics
a blanket of homeless
a hassle of bureaucrats
a pontification of columnists

HERPES A permanent case of the cooties, rendering the victim untouchable except by fellow sufferers, who must then spend their lives searching for each other like fireflies in the twilight.

HIGH BLOOD PRESSURE A potentially dangerous overinflation of the inner tubes, common in stressed individuals who lack a safety valve.

HIGH SCHOOL An institution that offers impressionable adolescents a first-rate education in sociology, esp. the dynamics of clique formation and pecking orders. Other subjects include Comparative Partying Techniques for Minors, Sex 101, Celibacy for Math and Science Wonks, Theory and Practice of Drag Racing, Pregnancy 101, Sports for Would-Be Studs (the key: avoid golf), Empty Rhetoric for Student Council

Aspirants, Male Bonding Through Social Alcoholism, and Living with Zits.

HIGH SOCIETY (archaic) A once-dominant breed of moneyed merrymakers whose lives centered around such curious customs as cotillions and ''coming out'' parties. Mainstay of old comedies set in the never-never land of 1920s Long Island, Manhattan or Connecticut, where elegant young women carefully dropped their *R*s and older ones lived in fear of the Marx Brothers. Now a scattered and vanishing tribe, best glimpsed by gate-crashing the graduation ceremonies at the Hotchkiss School or by scanning the *New York Times* marriage announcements for the Gentile names.

HIP Smartly attuned to the latest cutting-edge clichés.

HIPPIE A living fossil specimen from the late 1960s, formerly widespread but now confined in its habitat to selected rural hamlets where handicrafts and organic farming predominate; field marks include a luxuriant mane (now graying), scruffy plumage and a mellow demeanor that suggests continued familiarity with the weed *cannabis*.

HISTORIC DISTRICT A cluster of gracious old buildings permitted to survive as long as they can generate more revenue than the convention center proposed for the same site.

HISTORY The vast and thrilling pageant of human deeds and misdeeds through the ages, esp. as recorded by the lackeys of systematically oppressive male power elites. Now a moot point as the memory of our species gives way to computerized ROM and RAM—no relation to Romulus and Remus—and our span of consciousness dwindles to the electronic present.

HOMELESS, THE   Unsightly blemishes on the face of the city, easily ignored by averting one's glance.

HOMETOWN   The community that nurtures us during our formative years, so that we might attend a good school, succeed handsomely and spend the rest of our lives somewhere else.

HOOKER   A working woman commonly despised by people who sell themselves for even less.

HORSEY SET   The rusticating rich; a merry tribe of country folk who choose quadrupeds over pickup trucks as the favored means of locomotion, if only to distinguish themselves from their redneck neighbors beyond the white fence.

HOSPITAL   A bleak hotel that charges luxury rates for spartan rooms and notoriously bad cuisine; despite these and other shortcomings (e.g., the notable lack of a swimming pool and/or piano bar), many of the guests never leave.

HOSTAGE   A human being held captive in hope of extracting something in return, as practiced by terrorists, kidnappers and Saturday-morning toy advertisers during the Christmas season.

HOT DOG   A perennially popular American sausage containing an alarming conglomeration of former animal parts and by-products, causing justifiable suspicions about the nickname by which this particular sausage is so widely known.

HOT TUB   A steaming vat filled with bacteria, body oils and other exudations from the boiling flesh of one's fellow hedonists.

Houseplants Vegetable companions; pleasant green pets that rarely bite or throw up on the carpet.

Human Potential Movement Fast food for inner growth, California-style; a combination of mental reprogramming techniques and smile-button optimism that expunges any last vestige of renegade individuality, leaving us to think, speak and emote like replicants from some nightmarish sci-fi classic.

Human Resources Department Corporate nomenclature intended to confer greater dignity on personnel managers while reducing everyone else in the company to the status of bauxite or wood-pulp.

Humbug A fraudulence that offends common sense; also a quaint epithet that could be hurled more often at college faculty meetings, poetry readings, campaign speeches and new-age consciousness workshops.

Hunk A man freely viewed as a sex object by women who refuse to be viewed as such themselves, and generally aren't anyway.

Hype Fanfare for a flea.

Hyperactive Children A cheap and relatively clean energy source that might be put to good use after we deplete the planet's supply of fossil fuels.

Hyphenated Surnames The conjoining of family monickers in emulation of the gentry; a self-limiting disease that will terminate abruptly when, for example, Jason Smithers-Hershkowitz ties the knot with Tiffany Schnauzer-Chang.

HYPOCHONDRIA   One's own body viewed as a physiological minefield; a condition caused by overexposure to medical findings that link our social life, body type, bald spots or snoring habits to the increased likelihood of developing a fatal disease.

Ice Hockey A professionally staged brawl intermittently interrupted by the spectacle of men on skates chasing an oversized poker chip around an ice rink.

Identity Crisis When an intellectual realizes that the most profound influence on his mental development was "Looney Tunes."

Ideologue Typically an obscure humorless zealot who finds fulfillment by spouting the ideas of *famous* humorless zealots.

Illegal Aliens Expert swimmers who heroically volunteer for the least desirable jobs, thereby sparing unemployed Americans the degradation of underemployment.

IMPERIALISM The undue influence of a powerful nation over weaker ones; a charge traditionally leveled against the U.S. by radical foreign students who willingly surrender six months' allowance for a pair of American blue jeans.

IMPOTENCE An inopportune malfunction of the coupling mechanism in men, causing much mortification to the male ego, which in turn virtually assures future malfunctions of a similar nature.

IN-CROWD The Sultans of Snoot.

IN-LAWS A matching set of warm bodies acquired along with one's spouse as part of the matrimonial package; a team of natural adversaries in whom you may see reflected, as in a funhouse mirror, all the irritating quirks you had barely noticed in your beloved.

INBREEDING A grotesque magnification of undesirable traits caused by a lack of cross-pollination; a phenomenon occasionally encountered in isolated Appalachian communities, but more often observed at corporate board meetings, cat shows or Hollywood award ceremonies.

INCOME TAX Why our money is like a shirt that emerges from the wash two sizes smaller . . . or a homemade pie that pops out of the oven with a slice already missing . . . or a pound of hamburger that shrinks to the size of an Oreo cookie.

INFERIORITY COMPLEX The fatal self-doubt afflicting those who have witnessed too many examples of success in the media and not enough in their own lives . . . who have failed to see through the bravado of their equally insecure peers . . . and who have concluded that perhaps they actually *do* deserve to earn less than the used-car dealer whose idiotic commercial blares nightly from the TV.

INFLATION A monetary abundance that raises our salaries by *x* percent and the price of everything else by *x + 1* percent.

INFOMERCIAL A late-night talk show without commercial interruptions, offering hope for overweight women or balding men, companionship for lonely folks who are not too particular about the company they keep, and a chance for insomniacs to catch up on needed sleep.

INFORMATION HIGHWAY Where the telephone, television and computer merge onto a single high-tech turnpike, with tollbooths stationed at regular intervals. Where most of us will be spending our time if we wish to travel into the future, even though the real adventure and atmosphere will always be found on the back roads.

INNER CHILD The imprisoned spirit of our youthful selves; the little voice that from deep within us is heard to say, "This inner-child stuff is bunk!"

INNER CITY Where the outsiders live. A black ring on the urban dartboard, sandwiched between the white downtown bull's-eye and the equally white outer ring of suburbs. Anyone who lands there automatically forfeits all his points.

INSTANT REPLAY A sports fan's *déjà vu,* useful for savoring the great moments as well as the bonehead plays; a similar device in the minds of neurotics tends to rebroadcast more of the latter than the former, complete with a lifetime supply of nagging commentary.

INSTRUCTIONS All that stands between us and an ability to use our latest imported electronic gadget; an informative booklet written for those who don't understand modern technology, generally by those who don't understand English.

INSURANCE A form of gambling in which we bet against our chance of escaping disaster, and win only when we lose.

INTELLECTUAL A cerebral soul who values ideas over instincts . . . who would stand his ground during a stampede of woolly mammoths because they're theoretically extinct. For this reason relegated by society to harmless pursuits like grading term papers or formulating foreign policy.

INVESTMENT A fishing line baited with a herring in the hope of catching a marlin, which briefly flirts and tugs—then escapes with our offering in its belly, prompting us to stick another herring on the hook.

INTERACTIVE MEDIA That long-awaited opportunity to talk back to your TV, choose the commercials that pop onto your screen, and kill off an obnoxious sitcom character or two.

INTERNSHIP A sleepless ordeal imposed on young M.D.'s for the purpose of weeding out the weak and infirm among them, and eroding the health of the survivors sufficiently to ensure better empathy with their patients in the years to come.

92

INTERSTATE HIGHWAYS   An impressive asphalt circulatory system that enables a traveler to drive swiftly from Seattle to Miami without encountering a single landmark worth stopping for.

INTERVIEW   A face-to-face confrontation in which the object is to sell one's personal agenda before the droplets of sweat begin to bead visibly on the forehead; when they do, esp. during televised investigations of alleged scam artists, a camera is usually poised to roll in for a close-up.

IQ   The number that predicts the extent to which one will perform successfully on subsequent IQ tests.

IRONY   Watching ''Mr. Ed'' reruns with a knowing wink so that nobody will suspect we actually *like* ''Mr. Ed.'' A silky insincerity that commonly masks a morbid fear of being judged uncool.

IRRELEVANT   Anything that occurred before the first Baby Boomers climbed out of their playpens; e.g., the Treaty of Brest-Litovsk, the War of Jenkins' Ear, Zoroastrianism, the invention of the spinning jenny, cuneiform writing, the reign of Pepin the Short or the discovery of the Americas.

IVY LEAGUE   A confederacy of eight elite private universities that agree to play one another in football each year so that at least a few of them might emerge with winning teams. Notable for conferring lifelong prestige on their alumni and lifelong complexes on thousands of respectable students who never made it past the dean of admissions.

JALAPEÑO A potent Tex-Mex chili pepper that, if chomped boldly and rapidly enough, can for a few memorable seconds cause us to forget our woes, along with our name and zip code.

JARGON The prideful slang of the insider; an elaborate verbal disguise for commonplace ideas, used liberally to befuddle outsiders, secure the wink of approval from one's colleagues, and artificially inflate the stature of every profession from management to mortuary science.

JAZZ The musical language of glib twentieth-century urban sophisticates, created by the children of suffering nineteenth-century rural slaves.

JEANS Lower half of the international uniform of youth, the upper half being the zits.

JET SET Gypsies with money; a cosmopolitan clique of traveling hedonists who cultivate glamour at the expense of character. The high school in-crowd on a global scale.

JOB A state of employment everyone wants but few look forward to on a Monday morning; a demanding mate that frequently kills those who cannot love it.

JOCK A strapping young fellow who instinctively knows that his knack for teamwork and disdain for academics will someday catapult him into the corporate boardroom.

JOGGER Member of an ascetic cult given to public displays of self-abuse in city parks and along suburban thoroughfares; recognized by their monotonous low-stepping gait, expensive running shoes, visible disdain for mere pedestrians, and a tendency to keel over unexpectedly while celebrating their faith in their own endurance.

JUNK FOOD Cheap, satisfying, flavorsome victuals used as a substitute for real food and consisting mainly of salt, fat and sugar, deep-fried to bring out their full atherosclerotic potential.

JUNK MAIL A tidal wave of printed offers received with interest by approximately 2 percent of the target audience, which provides small consolation to the 98 percent of the trees that gave their lives in vain.

Junkie   An addict who spends inordinate amounts of money over a lifetime to support a habit like golfing, playing the lottery, eating cheese curls or collecting antique gumball machines.

Jury   A panel of amateurs called upon to decide life-or-death matters in court.

Keepsake A meaningful relic tucked away in a closet until we uncover it years later during an archaeological dig, by which time we've forgotten why we kept it.

Keyboard The hands-on portion of a harpsichord or a computer; the latter is often thoughtfully arranged so that the most critical keys are positioned next to DELETE.

Killer Bees Africa's revenge on the Americas.

Kindred Spirits Unrelated relatives whose souls bear an uncanny resemblance to our own. A precious commodity that dwindles as one drifts from the herd: cows and chickens enjoy them in abundance, as do jocks, M.B.A.'s, feminists and construction workers; but the stray individualist, uniquely warped by years of independent thinking and eccentric reading, may encounter them only in dreams.

Kitsch   Scholarly term that makes it acceptable for highbrows to enjoy lava lamps, lawn ornaments, blinking Jesus plaques, souvenir Empire State Buildings with thermometers down the front, or any other appealingly corny pop-culture icons that otherwise would be strictly *verboten*.

Kleptomaniac   One who steals for pleasure rather than material gain; a thief with breeding.

Kosher Deli   A cozy neighborhood food emporium that serves mountainous sandwiches of meat sanctified by clergymen if not by cardiologists.

Ku Klux Klan   Scientific name for the White-Hooded Redneck, a cocky but cowardly fowl that must gather in large flocks to prey upon individuals of supposedly inferior breeds.

LABORATORY ANIMALS Furry foot-soldiers drafted in the name of science. Some die nobly in the battle to eradicate cancer; others give their lives so that we might produce a peach-scented dandruff shampoo.

LADY (archaic) A gentle creature who spoke in melodious tones and wore a corset around her earthly desires, at least in public. A seriously endangered species, now approaching extinction as careerism and comedy clubs sweep across its former range.

LAWN The pride of suburbia: natural house-to-house carpeting, available only in a single shade of green. Must be trimmed weekly unless the owner intends to grow a miniature prairie, which supports a multitude of wildlife and billows wonderfully in the wind, but tends to incite class-action lawsuits by one's less imaginative neighbors.

LAWN ORNAMENTS Outdoor sculpture for the artistically innocent, who take pleasure in the contrasting tonalities of flamingo and grass, or in the robust texture of a painted plaster jockey with a ring through its nose.

LAWSUIT The attempted conversion of a personal grievance into a personal fortune; a contest generally won by the party that can afford to reimburse the lawyers on both sides of the dispute.

LAWYER A professional advocate hired to bend the law on behalf of a paying client; for this reason considered the most suitable background for entry into politics.

LECHER A stud with liver spots.

LECTURE CIRCUIT An opportunity for retired statesmen and aging authors to earn a secretary's yearly salary in a single day, thereby enabling them to approach the income bracket of an adolescent sitcom star.

LEFTIST A liberal who bites.

LEGALESE A richly convoluted dialect spoken by lawyers and used by them on important documents so that the rest of us have no choice but to hire their services as translators.

LEISURE The pleasant span of about fifteen minutes remaining to us after we recover from the ravages of the workday and before we nod off in our favorite chair.

LESBIAN   Quaint euphemism for a woman who resists the intrusion of a man into her private affairs but concurs with his taste in sex partners.

LEVERAGED BUYOUT   The gobbling of a big fish, often by a little fish with borrowed jaws.

LIBERAL   One who tolerates all beliefs and opinions except those with which he disagrees; a benevolent soul who advocates progressive measures for the sake of people with whom he would never associate.

LIBERAL ARTS   A family of academic disciplines embracing the sublimest achievements of humankind in literature, art, philosophy, music and statecraft through the ages; the traditional education for a lifetime of social maladjustment, periodic unemployment, teeth-gnashing and a wide range of underpaid careers.

LIFE EXPECTANCY   The span of years remaining before half the people our age are missing and presumed dead, possibly including ourselves.

LIFE SENTENCE   A bad career or a case of male-pattern baldness; also a prison term often commuted to a decade or so, suggesting that the "life" in question has been converted into dog-years for the convenience of the convict.

LINGERIE   Gossamer garments for the boudoir, designed not to be worn so much as removed. The amount of time t the garment stays on the wearer varies inversely with the amount of body surface b revealed by the garment, so that $t = 1/b$.

LIPOSUCTION A blubberectomy performed on those beyond hope of dieting; a surgical procedure from which the patient emerges significantly lighter in both pounds and dollars.

LIVER SPOTS The treason of the epidermis, revealing to the curious onlooker what dyed hair and face-lifts have attempted in vain to conceal.

LIVESTOCK Peaceful beasts who, like so many model employees, fail to see the chopping block in their future.

LOBBYISTS Political lounge lizards who practice their seductive arts in the halls of Congress.

LOBOTOMY A permanent numbing of the brain, generally accomplished through surgery but also attainable by watching any home shopping channel on a regular basis.

LOCH NESS MONSTER A publicity-shy *plesiosaur* said to lurk in the depths of a glacial Scottish lake and presumed to have so lurked for upward of sixty million years without benefit of jogging or oat bran.

LOITERING The crime of doing nothing in particular, particularly in public.

LONELINESS A fatal separation from kindred spirits, felt acutely by thoughtful souls in crowded shopping malls and corporate cafeterias; effectively remedied by reading a good book in solitude.

LONER An odd fellow who prefers his own follies to those of his neighbors, and procures for himself the freedom to develop into a genius, a nonentity or a chain-saw murderer.

Looks The primary criterion for social bonding in a society ruled by the mass media. Marriages tend to occur within the same aesthetically defined class, with beauty accruing to beauty and homeliness to homeliness—except for the occasional actress who mates with her business manager.

Looting A public shopping spree generously sponsored by local merchants in the wake of a riot.

Loser Anyone too incompetent to master the ways of the world, or too proud.

Lottery The equivalent of betting that the next pope will be from Duluth, or that the parrot in the pet-store window speaks Flemish.

Lower Middle Class Heaven for working-class folks who strive long and hard enough to purchase a small property, and hell for bright middle-class Baby Boomers who expected to coast through life on a liberal arts degree and their own wits.

Lowest Common Denominator In an unraveling social fabric, the few shared strands that still can be yanked by mass-media exploiters: sex, greed, fear of old age and fear of its alternative.

Loyalty (archaic) The noblest quality of a dog, a spouse, a friend, a ballplayer or an employee-company relationship. Nowadays the surest mark of a born patsy—including the dog, lately replaced as America's preferred pet by the ever-expedient cat.

Macho The strutting-and-crowing behavior of men who apparently use roosters as role models without ever wondering why there are so few of them in relation to hens.

Mafia A thriving but officially nonexistent network of family-run businesses specializing in vice, extortion, thuggery, racketeering, union manipulation and garbage removal. Also associated with the production and distribution of cement footwear.

MAIN STREET   A broad and imposing thoroughfare that generally runs through a district of empty storefronts.

MALE BONDING   A warm camaraderie developed by men through shared activities such as fishing, hunting, bowling, drinking, lynching, Jew-baiting, golf or gang warfare.

MALE-PATTERN BALDNESS   Cranial deforestation; a slow but inexorable retreat that cannot be reversed through lobbying or public fund-raising.

MALL RATS   Packs of gregarious teens stationed in shopping centers to provide free demonstrations of the latest punk fashions and attitudes.

MALPRACTICE   A serious charge of professional bungling commonly leveled against physicians but surprisingly not against incompetent stockbrokers, barbers, mechanics or millionaire ballplayers.

MANAGEMENT   A class of semi-skilled corporate hirelings whose rise within the organization correlates directly with the amount of work they delegate to their more talented underlings.

MAN-BASHING   Open season on the male of the species by especially bloodthirsty females; a shocking display of ingratitude toward the sex that invented nylon, the telephone and the chastity belt.

MARGARINE   A convenient butter substitute that enables us to clog our arteries without relying on animal fat.

MARIJUANA   A fragrantly burning weed that induces a giddy irreverence toward solemn authority figures, which probably explains why its possession is a criminal offense.

Market Share A coveted slice of a pie with green paper filling; the size of the slice varies as a product quashes the competition or is quashed in return.

Marriage A contract by which a free individual willingly enters into a state of bondage; compare MORTGAGE, which generally lasts longer.

Martial Arts A family of Asiatic self-defense disciplines consisting largely of sweeping ornamental gestures of the arms and legs; amusing to look at but disappointingly ineffective when one's opponent is armed with a semi-automatic.

Martini A noxious mixed beverage that used to be consumed over lunch by urban executives so they could take leave of their senses sufficiently to transact business. Today's cool predators require no artificial stimulants.

Masterpiece The latest opus by a commercially successful author or filmmaker, esp. as proclaimed by shrewd reviewers who like to see themselves quoted in national ad campaigns.

Math Anxiety An intense lifelong fear of two trains approaching each other at speeds of 60 and 80 mph.

M.B.A. Bearer of an academic credential untainted by the musty odor of great books, and therefore held in high esteem throughout the business world; usually hired to help convert thriving entrepreneurial companies into starchy bureaucracies.

M.D. A skilled mechanic who reaps vast sums in frequently futile attempts to repair defective parts.

MEDIA MOGUL A great octopus capable of winding its tentacles around profitable performers and publications thousands of miles away; also known to make quick getaways in a cloud of ink.

MELANCHOLY (archaic) The lyrical depression of a romantic, who used to find grace in suffering, and poignancy in unfulfilled longing. A major source of poetry since the invention of writing; an irrelevant emotion since the invention of Prozac.

MELTDOWN The point at which a deteriorating nuclear reactor, society or postal worker poses an immediate threat to humanity.

MEMO A generally pointless or self-evident message penned by management-level employees so as to avoid the unpleasantness of actual work.

MEMORIAL PARK The last resort; a peaceful destination wherein a body is content to rest forever, despite cramped accommodations, indifferent service and lackluster nightlife.

MEN'S MOVEMENT A positive offshoot of feminism, permitting oppressed males to grow emotionally by beating drums and wailing in the woods together.

MENIAL LABOR Lowest rung on the occupational ladder, with the next several rungs removed to assure greater climbing difficulty. The least esteemed of careers, probably because it leaves the mind free to roam.

MENTAL PATIENT   The ultimate status of freethinkers and other eccentrics with a deficit of adaptive elasticity; when rehabilitated and released after a regimen of shock treatments and mind-numbing drugs, they earn the lifelong title of *former* mental patient.

MENTOR   A kindly tutor who attempts to spare a young apprentice ten years of mistakes by imparting the accumulated wisdom from *thirty* years of mistakes.

MERGER   When $1 + 1 = 1$, with the remainder going on unemployment.

METEOROLOGIST   A high-tech weather prognosticator whose accuracy you may usually surpass by sticking your head out the window.

METHOD ACTING   A school of thespianism that encourages performers to overstudy their roles until all traces of crowd-pleasing spontaneity, humor and sentiment are successfully expunged. A solemn search for the motivation behind a sneeze, or the rationale for drinking a cup of tea.

METRICS   A universal system of measurements that threatens to make everything in the world neatly divisible by 10, although its proponents somehow neglected to split our time into *centidays* and *millidays*. The despair of poetry lovers who must now consider that Robert Frost actually had ''kilometers to go'' before he slept. The bane of history teachers who must tell their awed students that Abraham Lincoln stood 1.93 m in his stocking feet. A contagion long and bravely resisted by the American people, most of whom still believe that an ounce of prevention is worth 0.4536 kg of cure.

MICROWAVE OVEN   A timesaving kitchen appliance that doubles as a containment device for exploding chickens and small household pets.

MIDDLE AMERICA   The vast mid-region of the American land and spirit; a happy valley unclouded by ideas, romance, art or poignancy, and therefore hospitable to the proliferation of shopping malls, twig-shaded housing tracts, power mowers and acres of wall-to-wall carpeting.

MIDDLE CLASS   The vanishing breed of comfortable, unpretentious burghers who dominated the American scene at mid-century, when, according to several reliable reports, a single moderate income could actually buy a presentable house in the suburbs—with money left over for a station wagon, college tuition, a Sears wardrobe for Dad and homemade dresses for Mom.

MIDLIFE CRISIS   The sickening realization, usually at the onset of middle age, that we've spent the past twenty years buttoning up into the wrong buttonholes.

MIGRANT WORKERS   The temps of agriculture; brave and desperate toilers commonly enslaved by latter-day plantation masters, who cleverly charge them slightly more for a week's food and lodging than they pay them for picking a week's worth of oranges.

MILITANT   A political beggar with the attitude of a generalissimo.

MIME   A harmless public nuisance whose silence creates a pretense of profundity for crowds of onlookers who pretend to enjoy the show.

MINIMALISM   The anorexic sensibility as perpetrated on late twentieth-century literature, music, painting and sculpture; pallid humorless art that shuns exuberance as a vegetarian shuns roast beef.

MINIMUM SECURITY PRISON   A residential athletic club for white-collar criminals, who enjoy a better standard of living in captivity than the average ghetto-dweller does at liberty.

MINORITY GROUP   Any social class whose members feel they have less power than they deserve, and which, when added to all other such groups, amounts to 100 percent of the population.

MIRACLE   A report of a holy visage appearing on a window shade, or of a marketing manager reading Shakespeare for pleasure.

MIRROR   A truthful reflector shunned by vampires, hypocrites and aging fashion models.

MOBSTER   An aggressive businessman with bad taste in suits and a penchant for outgunning the competition.

MODERATE   A rational soul who attempts to live peacefully on the land between the opposing trenches of a battlefield. At least one such individual, made cranky by the perpetual crossfire, has retaliated against both camps by writing a satirical dictionary.

MODERN ARCHITECTURE   A blight of colossal boxes that, from the 1950s through the 1970s, mysteriously sprouted and proliferated in the business districts of cities throughout the civilized world, making them visually interchangeable—and aesthetically uninhabitable—for centuries to come.

MODERNISM   The cultural movement that trashed the smug optimism of the Victorians for a more fashionable pose of smug nihilism.

MORALITY   A traditional code of decency that went out the window about the same time as belief in eternal damnation.

MORTGAGE   How banks enlist would-be property owners as indentured servants for a period of twenty to thirty years or until death, whichever comes first.

MOTEL   A convenient roadside inn that shelters tired travelers and libidinous locals.

MOTIVATIONAL SEMINAR   Where would-be achievers discover that the best way to improve their lot is to start a seminar business.

MOTORCYCLE   The devil's preferred mode of transport. A noisy, fuel-propelled bike without training wheels, favored by those for whom automobiles provide insufficient risk to life and limb.

MOVIES   The preeminent storytelling medium of our time, heir to the novel, the epic poem, the folk tale and the drawing of a bison-hunting expedition on a cave wall. A happy excuse to cuddle in a darkened room while your arm falls asleep and your shoes go *skraaack* as you pull them off the floor.

MOVIE STARS   America's contribution to the pantheon of world mythology: the fabled hat-check girls and soda jerks who attained immortality on a two-dimensional screen while their three-dimensional bodies went the way of all flesh. Recent generations have appeared decidedly less godlike but more resistant to decay, thanks to daily workouts and regular visits to the plastic surgeon.

MUD-WRESTLING A degrading women's sport developed, curiously enough, since the advent of the feminist movement.

MUGGER A benevolent citizen of the streets who frequently spares the lives of total strangers in exchange for any cash and valuables in their possession.

MULTICULTURALISM The reasonable notion that a Navajo medicine man can tell us just as much about human nature as Homer or Rembrandt, coupled with the equally valid belief that today's students will prefer the medicine man.

MUSIC VIDEO How film-school cinematographers and posturing postpubescent stars collaborated to keep rock music on artificial life support long after it should have died naturally.

MUTANTS Creatures with aberrant genes who suddenly appear on the scene, as if from another planet; e.g., fanatical adventurers who climb sheer rock walls with no visible means of support, or executives who actually enjoy working eighteen-hour days.

MYSTERY NOVEL Murder among the upper crust regarded as a source of pleasure by a peculiarly voracious segment of the reading public.

Narcotic Anything habit-forming that dulls the senses and induces sleep, like an all-night cable news program or a Henry James novel; less addictive alternatives include college economics textbooks and insurance salesmen.

National Anthem In the U.S., a rousing hymn widely criticized for its martial spirit, but more likely reviled for the unattainable high notes that cause such mortification to those who sing it, especially when strangers are present; at baseball games, generally rendered as a soul ballad, with approximately three times the number of syllables as the lyricist had in mind.

NATIONAL PARK   A primeval wilderness set aside by the government for invasion by armies of rabid vacationers.

NATURAL FIBERS   The threads favored by fashionable young people who prefer their wrinkles to be confined to their clothing; also popular with older folks who hope those wrinkles will make their faces look pristine by comparison.

NATURAL SELECTION   The reproductive screening process by which the gods determine whose genes will represent the future of the species, based solely on a proclivity for fruitful sex; a phenomenon that does not bode well for monks, nerds, women with ticking clocks, reclusive scholars, a significant percentage of interior decorators, and other mild-mannered gentlefolk. Proof positive that Providence favors the lusty over the learned, and that human evolution will eventually return us to our rowdy Paleolithic roots.

NEAR-DEATH EXPERIENCE   The light at the end of the tunnel, reported as reassuring evidence of a hereafter by people who have danced on the edge of eternity and lived to tell about it; unfortunately we have yet to hear any reliable reports from the folks who have actually plunged over the brink.

NECKTIE   A decorative noose worn by businessmen.

NEGOTIATING   The art of persuading your opponent to take the nice shiny copper penny and give you the wrinkled old paper money.

NEIGHBORS   The strangers who live next door.

NEON LIGHT   The symbol of modern urban nightlife: a twisted tube that glows seductively and contains nothing but gas.

NERD   A poor ungainly misfit, usually a male adolescent, who is scorned and ostracized by his peers for failure to cultivate a sexually knowing persona—until he graduates from engineering school and secures his first job at twice their salary. One who finds refuge in personal computers and ranks mathematics above style in the eternal hierarchies.

Also: **GEEK**   A nerd without mathematical aptitude.

NERVOUS BREAKDOWN   The overwinding of a wristwatch; the snapping of a rubber band; the slipping of a fan belt; the unraveling of a yo-yo; a malfunction known to occur in higher primates who agonize endlessly over mental abstractions, when they should be out picking bananas and frolicking in the trees.

NETWORKING   The art of socializing with people you detest so that you might be able to work with them in the near future.

NEUROTIC   Sane but unhappy about it.

NEW AGE   The illegitimate offspring of a spiritual liaison between California and the Orient; a system of nebulous beliefs and therapies centering on a philosophy that may be summarized as follows: "God is love; I love; therefore I am God."

NEW YORK INTELLECTUALS   A moribund Manhattan-based tribe of deep thinkers whose members effectively cornered the market on moral indignation throughout the mid-twentieth century. Stern guardians of leftist orthodoxy and chastisers of the Philistines.

NIRVANA   The ultimate extinction of the individual soul; a transcendent state sought by Hindus and Buddhists through right living, although it may be attained more easily by working for a Japanese corporation.

NONCONFORMIST   A conformist with a relatively obscure role model.

NONSEXIST LANGUAGE   The neutering of our vocabulary to gratify feminist sensibilities. Examples: *chairperson, ombudsperson, henchperson, Founding Parents, cattlepersons and Indians, "O Absalom, my offspring, my offspring!"*

NOSE JOB   Cosmetic truncation of a prominent proboscis, commonly performed on upscale adolescents as a rite of passage and deliverance from the bonds of ethnicity; the attempted suppression of a genetic heritage that, to the chagrin of everyone involved, tends promptly to reassert itself in the next generation.

NOVEL   A bundle of truths couched in several hundred pages of lies. An archaic form of entertainment still enjoyed by patient armchair enthusiasts, who gladly surrender a month or more of their lives for the chance to inhabit an artificial world. Persists today in various incarnations both high and low; the former are useful as filler for remainder catalogs, while the latter tend to become successful TV miniseries.

NOVELIZATION   The metamorphosis of a successful bad movie into an even worse book, which typically outsells the *original* book on which the movie was based.

NUCLEAR FALLOUT   The powdery airborne residue of an exploded atomic bomb, which if touched or inhaled will make short work of anyone spared by the actual blast.

NUDITY   A generally sensuous state of undress in a painting, photograph, motion picture or perfume ad, as opposed to *naked-ness*, which is something glimpsed at a nudist colony.

NURSING HOME   A banishing-place for aged citizens who in less enlightened times would have been granted a place of honor in the homes of their children.

OBESITY An overabundance of lard carried about the human frame; a condition particularly common throughout the rural backwaters of the land, among unfashionable folks too emotionally secure to waste their lives dieting.

OBITUARY A final summation of our lives that, for most of us, occupies about three inches of space in what will shortly become cage liner for our neighbor's parakeet.

OFFICE   A clean, functional, brightly lit cell inhabited five days a week by diligent souls who forfeit their lives to make a living.

OFFICE POLITICS   A system of secret alliances, treacherous intrigues, backstabbings and petty rivalries designed to relieve the tedium of corporate life. The chief legacy of Byzantine civilization in the Western world, appropriately modified for our times; instead of blinding or maiming one's rivals, one simply mutilates their egos.

OIL   The flammable liquid residue of fossilized prehistoric plants and beasts, found to be suitable for fueling engines and Middle East conflicts.

OLD-BOY NETWORK   Male bonding for profit, esp. as practiced by former school chums and their cronies. Not to be confused with male prostitution.

OPPRESSED   Laid low by CRAMPs (Capitalist Racist American Male Patriarchalists).

ORGAN DONOR   Someone who looks forward to being outlived by his liver.

ORGANICALLY GROWN   Nurtured on animal excreta for greater appeal to environmentally correct consumers.

ORGASM   The punchline some women just don't get, generally because their mates have a tendency to rush through the joke. Other women *pretend* to get it, and still others demand to hear it again and again.

OSTRACISM   The systematic shunning of one who defies the taboos of an in-group, as practiced by the ancient Athenians, the

Amish, West Point cadets and modern academic literary circles, esp. when a fellow scholar confesses to an admiration of Joyce Kilmer's "Trees."

Out-of-body Experience (OBE) An extrasensory form of travel that thrills the questing soul, although it diminishes the likelihood of returning with decent snapshots.

Outdoor Sculpture Unnatural configurations of scrap metal deposited in city parks, college campuses and other urban oases, at the precise locations where they are most likely to obliterate an idyllic vista.

Overachiever A swan who was happier as an ugly duckling.

Overkill Possessing more than enough to wipe out the opposition, as with nations that stockpile nuclear devices, celebrities who collect Rolls-Royces like matchbook covers, and anyone who picks up a Harvard law degree to go with a Harvard M.B.A.

Ozone Layer The earth's own sunscreen, now dwindling sufficiently over the polar regions to produce fried penguins in the south and baked Alaskans up north.

PACKAGE TOUR A professionally planned vacation designed to sustain the reassuring illusion that one has never left home; a feat accomplished by housing the travelers in familiar hotel chains, conveying them on air-conditioned buses, and keeping them in the company of captive fellow tourists who all resemble Uncle Harry and Aunt Marge.

PACKAGING The glossy outer wrap that can sell us on a second-

rate product, which explains why so many corporate job appli-
cants and aspiring politicians take refuge inside it.

PAPARAZZI   Pesky flies that swarm around the meatier celebrities, taking an occasional bite before being flattened by a timely
swat of the tail.

PARANOIA   The pathological belief that one is *important* enough
to be the object of a conspiracy.

PARASITE   A base creature that extracts a living from the lives of
others, like a tapeworm or a biographer.

PARENTING   Raising children, esp. by consenting adults of
heightened consciousness and sensitivity. Gerund form of the
verb *to parent,* conjugated in the present indicative as follows:

I parent	we parent
thou parentest	you parent
he she } parents it	they parent

PARK   A picturesque parcel of landscaping set aside by cities
for use by muggers, drug dealers, squirrels and habitual sex
offenders.

PARKING LOT   Where we spend a quarter of an hour searching
for a well-situated space so that we can avoid walking sixty
seconds to the mall entrance.

Parking Meter   An outdoor slot machine that takes our spare change but never delivers a jackpot; when the word EXPIRED appears in the window, the house collects from *us*.

Pasta   Concentrated carbohydrates of Italo-Chinese ancestry; available in a profusion of shapes, sizes and fashionable colors, all of which taste like macaroni.

Pedigree   The genealogy of the family dog, attesting to its ethnic purity and illustrious lineage, including, perhaps, a grandsire who barked at the Second Battle of Bull Run, or a great-aunt who chewed the leg of Hubert Humphrey's favorite chair. A piece of documentation much prized by people of mixed ancestry who don't know the names of their own great-grandparents.

Peer Pressure   That which a lemming experiences on the brink of a seaside cliff.

Pendulum   A shifting weight that in America swings from puritanism to paganism, from banality to brutality—without ever coming to rest in the middle.

Penny Stock   An opportunity for investors to get in on the ground floor moments before the elevator descends to the basement.

Performance Artist   A street loonie with a foundation grant.

Performing Arts   Culture on the half shell, a dish much loved by bourgeois patrons who relish the chance to flaunt expensive clothes and applaud their own elevated tastes in public.

Personal Ad   Lnly S/D W/B M/F sks lv & cmpnshp w intel, prof, Ivy-educ, sxy, phys fit, emot & fin sec prsn who enjs Wdy Aln flms & sq dncg, wch xplns why S/D W/B M/F is stl lnly.

PERSONAL COMPUTER Man's best friend for the postcanine era: a gentle, undemanding companion who demonstrates infinite patience with our mental limitations . . . who never criticizes our table manners or maligns us in front of the neighbors . . . and who asks only that we provide it with a sturdy table, an electrical outlet and, every so often, a major project to eat.

PESTICIDE A noxious chemical preparation designed to poison any animal having the audacity to attack a vegetable.

PERSONAL GROWTH See TUMOR.

PERSONAL ORGANIZER A portable calendar that constantly reminds compulsive souls how overworked they are, to no avail.

PETRI DISH A miniature arena in which one may observe the effect of toxins upon a living culture. See also TELEVISION.

PH.D. A good doctor whose writing and lecturing style successfully cures the average student of any hunger for knowledge.

PHEROMONES Sexually compelling scents wafted into the air by primitive creatures to lure potential mates from great distances, as may be witnessed in Florida during spring break.

PHILISTINE The uncouth bully who knocks the glasses off the sensitive little bookworm, then proceeds to outearn him, outlive him and have more fun in the process.

PHOBIA A minor form of cowardice peculiar to the age of specialization, when elevators, bridges, cats and cobwebs are capable of inflicting terrors that used to be reserved for imminent death and eternal damnation.

PHOTOJOURNALIST   A paparazzo with a college degree.

PIMP   Agent and business manager for a lady of the streets; a natural entrepreneur who rents out captive human beings for profit, then spends his fortune on ornamental hats.

PIZZA   A giant communion wafer shared by celebrants of the great god Gluttony, generally after prolonged disputations concerning the nature and number of the holy toppings.

PLAGIARISM   Failure to adorn stolen ideas with footnotes, as opposed to scholarship, which repeatedly acknowledges the theft.

PLASTIC   That which never decays, even when we want it to; a cheap universal substitute for wood, metal, paper, cloth, human flesh and other archaic natural materials that tend to go bad. Atoms of this substance (listed as *Ps* on the Periodic Table) are thought to possess a half-life exceeding the span of time remaining to our solar system, but in all likelihood nobody will be around to verify this theory in person.

PLEA BARGAIN   The willingness of the law to forgive a criminal who is also a stool pigeon.

PLUMBER   Owner of the largest house in the neighborhood, which conveniently enables his wife and children to retreat beyond smelling range after he returns from his rounds.

PMS   An uncontrollable monthly mayhem. See WEREWOLF.

POETRY, MODERN

> word puzzles
> > > (without solutions)
> > arranged in short   uneven
> > lines (without
> > > > punctuation)
> by fractured
> > > souls
> > (without   mercy)
> > > so that weeeeeeeeeee
> the readers (without
> a clue)
> > > might experience
> stark Profundity (without
> > > > snickering)
> > or kiss the bitter lips of
> > > > > Madness
> > > (without gargling)

POLICE   Roving officers whose eternal vigilance curbs the public tendency to commit mischief; generally hired by the municipality, although the brightest opportunities in the field now belong to the self-appointed—esp. for the following job descriptions:

Position	Primary Activity
Public Health Police	Castigate smokers in front of their spouses and children
PC Police	Round up loose-lipped speakers and writers on college campuses
First Amendment Police	Root out and dismantle public Nativity scenes and similar threats to freedom
Personal Hygiene Police	Lecture wayward citizens who forget to use underarm deodorant

POLITICAL BOSS A miracle worker capable of raising the dead on Election Day.

POLITICALLY CORRECT TERMINOLOGY Inadvertently comical euphemisms mandated by committees of humorless academicians for the purposes of offending no group except believers in free speech.

Examples	Translation
Abundantly capitalized individual	Rich man
Financially challenged individual	Poor man
Self-employed outdoor monetary solicitor	Beggar man
Personal-property appropriation specialist	Thief

POLITICIAN A bundle of gaseous ambition cleverly packaged as a public servant or a corporate sales manager.

POLYESTER   An unnatural fiber used to construct inexpensive wrinkle-free garments widely favored by the masses; despised by the knowing elite precisely because said garments are so favored by such people.

POP CULTURE   Heir to the defunct civilization of Western Christendom; possibly the first culture democratic enough to reflect the popular preference for bad taste over beauty. The source of virtually all learned references in contemporary conversation; e.g., "I'll get you, my pretty—and your little *dog*, too!"

POP MUSIC   Short for *popular music* (i.e., the music of the people), created by reclusive millionaires in collaboration with owlish sound technicians; as opposed to "unpopular music," which consists mainly of classical, folk and bagpipe.

PORNOGRAPHY   A two-dimensional substitute for that which the consumer cannot accomplish in three.

POSEUR   A Shakespearean scholar who pretends to be a fitness instructor so he can pick up women at singles bars.

POSITIVE THINKING   Self-improvement through self-deception.

POST-CHRISTIAN ERA   The historical epoch we entered as Jesus lost most of his following to the deified Elvis, who is believed to have produced more gold records during his career.

POSTAL WORKER   A container labeled CONTENTS UNDER PRESSURE, slowly heated over a fire by illiterate supervisors.

POSTLITERACY   Humankind's return to its normal state of simian bliss following the prolonged aberration of the print era.

POSTMODERN ARCHITECTURE Notable for enlivening the monumental sterility of modern architecture with a welcome dose of warped humor.

POVERTY The unadorned life; a state of material deprivation calmly endured by primitive tribes, idealized by pastoral poets and fervently embraced by holy men. In the consumer age, one of the chief causes of human misery.

POWDER ROOM Where women retreat in pairs to swap intimate secrets about their men, who, left together at the table, use their five minutes of freedom to talk baseball.

POWER The ability to make our fellow humans squirm, sweat and stammer on command. Often regarded as an aphrodisiac; actually a potent laxative that, whenever ingested by people in high places, causes everyone below to run for cover.

POWER BROKER The man who hands out the laxatives.

POWERBOAT An obtrusive waterborne craft designed to infuse the tranquillity of wilderness lakes with something of the city's noise and pollution, so as to engender a more familiar environment for affluent urban weekenders.

PREJUDICE A lamentable inclination to denounce all pit bulls as ruffians, on the basis of tooth marks from just one or two bellicose individuals.

PREPPIE End-product of the American private-school system, typically identified by lockjaw speech, a predilection for tweeds and table manners, an inclination toward the nautical and other amiable eccentricities that qualify one for automatic membership in the nation's ruling class.

Press, The   In the U.S., a freewheeling clan of news scribes who unofficially elect a President every four years, then conspire to drive him from office.

Prime Time   The precious evening hours of our lives that most of us spend watching TV.

Pro-Choice   Choosing to let a woman choose, as distinguished from choosing that choice oneself; a position that may be deftly defended without even using the A-word.

    Ant. **Pro-Life**   A label that accurately reflects the position of its adherents, except with regard to certain individuals who run abortion clinics.

Pro Football   The primary cause of wife abandonment by American males, who sit spellbound before the tube as teams of faceless hulks try to outdo each other in generating offense.

Pro Wrestling   A form of theater dedicated to the preservation of our Neanderthal heritage.

Producer   The crass cigar-chewer who stands behind all the airy illusions of the movies, like the wizard behind the curtain.

Productivity   The accomplishment of more work in less time; an arbitrary goal for which corporate underlings risk their health and equilibrium so that their bosses might pacify the speculators who gamble with the company's stock.

Profanity   The eloquence of the gutter; a rhetorical shortcut to persuasion in the absence of persuasive ideas. An effective device for bolstering poorly written screenplays and stand-up comedy routines, esp. if repeated often enough and loudly enough to wear down the resistance of the audience.

PROFESSIONAL MODEL Cheekbones that sell cosmetics; hipbones that sell anorexia.

PROFIT SHARING A corporate scheme to line the pockets of upper-echelon employees in accordance with the biblical motto ''To him that hath, more shall be given.''

PROGRESS The public illusion that everything is getting better and better, coupled with the private suspicion that it's only getting more and more complicated.

PROPAGANDA Patriotism as practiced by our enemies.

PROPERTY VALUES Suburban euphemism for ''Let's keep this neighborhood lily white.''

PSYCHIC In the tabloid press, a self-proclaimed soothsayer who publishes annual predictions for a credulous public; e.g., that a volcano will erupt near Perth Amboy, New Jersey . . . or that a nervous alien will be seen ordering thirty-five Big Macs in Albuquerque . . . or that Elvis will run for the Ohio state assembly under an assumed name . . . or that a member of the British royal family will give birth to a miniature forty-one-year-old optometrist. The lowbrow equivalent of the stock market forecasters who infest public TV, except that nobody saves their predictions to review at year's end.

PSYCHOANALYSIS Allowing one's mind to be dismantled like the temple of Abu Simbel, then paying for the privilege of reassembling it oneself on higher and safer ground. An expensive upper-middle-class hobby often pursued over a lifetime, esp. if the analyst is shrewd enough to hide a few of the parts.

PSYCHOBABBLE   The jargon of standardized introspection, favored esp. by chronic talk-show guests and victims of terminal therapy.

PUBERTY   The age at which most humans jettison their genius and start revving up their genes.

PUBLIC RELATIONS   Propaganda for hire.

PUBLICITY   The theory that no news is bad news, that neither divorce nor adultery nor sex videotapes nor checking into the Betty Ford Clinic will stay our celebrities from swiftly cashing in on the free exposure.

PUBLISHING   Formerly the one indispensable private enterprise in any civilized society; now a minor appendage of the entertainment industry.

PUNDIT   One who is paid to offer the world his opinions, as distinguished from those who offer them gratis on city sidewalks.

PUNK MOVEMENT   The attempt by certain disaffected adolescents of the 1980s to gain status by rendering themselves even more unattractive than they were originally.

PUSHER   The underground apothecary; a street-corner druggist who must continually extend his business to new customers as his old ones expire.

Put-down   A species of sarcastic insult freely exchanged among friends, colleagues and TV sitcom characters, esp. since the extinction of dueling.

Pyramid Scheme   The recruiting of recruits to recruit still more recruits, so that a mid-level recruit may theoretically amass a fortune once the entire population of the inhabited universe has been recruited.

Quack **1.** The sound of a duck call. **2.** What an unsound doctor is called as he ducks out of town.

Quagmire Any situation more easily entered into than exited from; e.g., a guerrilla war, a bad marriage or a conversation with an insurance salesman.

Quality of Life What an industrialized nation is said to offer when enough of its citizens are suffering from terminal stress.

Quiche A rich and highly caloric egg pie, once consumed almost exclusively by the French peasantry, then discovered by gourmets, who introduced it to the upwardly mobile crowd and thus procured for it a fatal popularity. Now a staple at company cafeterias and roadside hash houses, where it is rapidly descending in status toward its primeval roots.

QUOTA   The color-by-numbers approach to resolving social inequities.

QUOTATION   A line borrowed from some immortal work of the dominant culture, generally in an effort to impress one's peers.
  Examples:

"I think, therefore I am."
  —Descartes

"It was the best of times, it was the worst of times."
  —Dickens

"Nyuk-nyuk-nyuk."
  —Curly

R & B Streetwise black son of the blues, and unwitting father of a screaming child called rock 'n' roll. The child passed for white, made a quick fortune and promptly forgot its old man.

R & D Breezy nickname for Research and Development; an intellectual ghetto within the American corporation, populated by rival gangs of Ph.D.'s who carry pocket protectors at all times. Not to be confused with R & B.

Rabid Foaming ominously at the mouth, like a mad dog or an activist on either side of the abortion issue.

Radio In its primitive days, a magic box that transported listeners to wondrous realms of comedy and imagination; now a source from which we select background noise targeted to our personal market demographics.

Radio Call-in Show An outlet for the frustrations of average Americans who otherwise might climb to the nearest rooftop and start picking off pedestrians with an Uzi.

Rain Forest What environmentalists call what remains of what used to be known as the *jungle*; the vanishing abode of Tarzan, his apes, 2,278,303 exotic species and most of the oxygen on this planet. Make that 2,278,302 exotic species . . . 2,278,301 . . .

Rap A pounding headache set to rhythm; a profane street sermon; the end of music as we know it.

Rat Race Popular metaphor used to depict the Darwinian struggle for survival, esp. in the business world; a lifelong marathon in which the laurels go to the fastest and cleverest rats.

Reactionary A sentimental curmudgeon for whom the past is perfect, the present tense, and the future extremely conditional.

Real Estate A small piece of the earth traded as a speculative commodity for centuries after some dead white male had the audacity to claim ownership. Each parcel commands a price based on its perceived value, so that a hundred-acre stand of spruce forest fetches roughly as much as the weed-infested lot next to a video store.

RECESSION What the government calls a depression that spares the rich.

RECYCLING The meticulous separation of one's trash into its fundamental components, so as to conserve precious natural resources like glass and plastic.

REDNECK Popular term for a rustic male, but rarely employed when addressing one in person; a specimen of humanity typically encountered by urban motorists arrested for obscure reasons along sweltering country highways.

REFRIGERATOR A communal coffin for decomposing animal and vegetable carcasses and parts thereof; the centerpiece of every American home.

REFUGEES Oppressed individuals who flee an intolerable situation to start a new life, like middle-class New Yorkers who quit their murderous jobs and move to Vermont.

REINCARNATION A chance for the likes of Napoleon, Joan of Arc, Kafka and Cleopatra to be reborn as shipping clerks, receptionists, morticians and beauty consultants.

RELATIONSHIP What men and women started having together after the demise of romance; a liaison that commences with mutual lust and normally ends with mutual disgust.

RELATIVITY An elaborate theory of space, time, mass and energy understood by approximately fourteen people, nine of whom are already dead. Part of the theory explains why, for example, a hedgehog tossed straight up on a moving train appears to fall straight down to a passenger, but to an outside observer seems to describe an arc; it may also be extrapolated to explain why our salaries appear to be shrinking, especially in relation to those of major league baseball players.

REPRESSED Sitting on one's inner demon to keep it decorously immobilized, as practiced by lifelong Presbyterians or anyone who attempts to exchange pleasantries with a tyrannical boss.

REPUTATION An edifice that takes half a lifetime to build and just one seismic blip to reduce to rubble.

RESIGN What a PR-sensitive organization forces a fired official to do so that it can profess "deep regret" over the incident.

RESTAURANT In New York and Hollywood, a public conference room frequented by media heels making deals over meals.

RÉSUMÉ See FICTION.

RETIREMENT The liberation of a captive butterfly just as its wings begin to crumble.

RETIREMENT VILLAGE A pleasant ghetto to which the elderly voluntarily commit themselves as a means of escape from inflated rents, muggers, diabolical children, loneliness and other pestilences of the world they formerly inhabited.

REVISIONIST HISTORY Dressing the past in the political fashions of the present; e.g., Robin Hood, who not long ago would have been hailed by academics as a progressive proponent of socialist wealth redistribution, now becomes a sociopathic, patriarchalist

DWEM (Dead White European Male) and systematic despoiler of wildlife resources, with a phallocentrist affinity for violence and meat ingestion.

REVOLUTION An attempt to stimulate new growth on an old tree by lopping off all its limbs.

REVOLUTIONARY An oppressed person waiting for the opportunity to become an oppressor.

RIOT A bloody rampage by overheated youths in response to bad news, like an unfavorable jury verdict, or good news, like a *favorable* jury verdict.

ROADKILL The proverbial pot-luck special at the local drive-in restaurant; a rare treat for anyone who has never tasted raccoon burgers or porcupine *cordon bleu*.

ROBOT In Japan, an automaton programmed to carry out demeaning, repetitive tasks that in America are assigned to assembly-line workers.

ROCK 'N' ROLL A raucous musical rendering of adolescent glandular activity, peddled to receptive teens since the 1950s as a cheap and relatively bloodless means of overthrowing parental authority—along with most of the accumulated values of Western civilization.

ROCK CONCERT Where the young gather in astonishing numbers to follow a degenerate Pied Piper with amplifiers.

ROLE MODEL One whose character traits are found worthy of emulation by impressionable young people; e.g., professional athletes, rock and video idols with distinctive hair, sullen postpubescent movie actors, drug dealers and anyone else with a seven-figure income. In less-advanced societies, the list would include statesmen, writers, scientists and scholars.

ROMANCE NOVEL   A woman's recurring dream of being abducted while wearing a period costume, generally by a dashing fellow who bears not the faintest resemblance to her husband.

ROOTS   Deep bonds that anchor a living thing to its native turf and nurture it for life; a feature noticeably absent in yuppies and tumbleweeds.

RUDENESS   The etiquette of the Rock era.

RUG   A decorative woolly patch used to conceal a bare expanse of wooden floor or head. The latter style rarely has an Oriental design woven into it and almost never needs vacuuming; both types tend to slide around unless anchored securely.

RUINS   The forlorn architectural remains of a once-mighty civilization, like the walls of Babylon or the downtown district of any average American city.

RUST BELT   The aging heart of the republic, now in the terminal stages of coronary disease; a grim northern realm of blackened brick mills and foundries, blackened snow, blackened lungs and blackened spirits; the faded empire of coal, steel, railroads and other industries now dead or wheezing; a province more deserted than entered into, as its citizens depart for southern climes or that great coke oven in the sky.

RUTHLESS   Exhibiting all the tender solicitude of a mother guppy or a corporate takeover specialist.

SADOMASOCHISM The employment of chains, handcuffs, whips, blindfolds, bedposts and/or Nazi uniforms as instruments of love.

SAILING An aqueous pastime pursued by men of means who relish the prospect of being blown out to sea on a Sunday afternoon. Also an obscure Anglo-Saxon dialect spoken by such hobbyists, consisting largely of phrases like ''Hoist the thwizzlejib'' and ''Squinch the starboard squallnoggin.''

Salad Bar A sunny smorgasbord of fresh leafy vegetables, legumes, raw fungi and other low-calorie treats designed to pacify perpetual dieters, who promptly anoint their selections with dollops of creamy blue cheese dressing.

Salary A market value assigned to professionals as a function of their scarcity, their usefulness to employers and their ability to feign enthusiasm for their work.

Sale An opportunity to spend $199 on a $199 coat whose retail price has temporarily been jacked to $300.

Salivation The involuntary physiological response of Pavlov's dogs to the dinner bell, an investment banker to a company ripe for takeover, or a fundamentalist preacher to an unsaved sinner (See also SALVATION).

Salvation That which spares a vulnerable soul the discomfort of the fiery pit so that it may endure an eternity of harp music.

Sanitation Worker The title conferred on garbage men when they started earning more than public-school teachers.

Santa Claus The rotund, red-suited gentleman who embodies all that is magical and good, and whose inevitable demise drives many of his young mourners into lifelong careers as cynics.

Satanism Rooting for the Evil One simply because his team has taken a late-inning lead. A dark, sacrificial cult frequently practiced by bored and secretive teenagers; somewhat less popular among the chickens, children and household pets whose body parts are used in their rituals.

Schizophrenia Not the proverbial split personality, but a long retreat from life's battles and unpleasantness into a shadow-world where the trees have ears, and dogs recite "Hiawatha" in a Swedish accent; considered pathological except among modern poets and performance artists, in whom it may be regarded as the norm.

School A refuge for small fry: growing children, minnows or minor artists with interchangeable styles.

Science Fiction Fairy tales for nerds.

Secular Humanism The belief that man created such wondrous works as Parcheesi and insect repellant without divine intervention, and therefore deserves to be revered as a god; a view hotly disputed by fundamentalists, who insist that only a wise and beneficent Providence could have inspired the invention of wax lips.

Segregation In an earlier era, the government enforcement of that which now occurs naturally at golf tournaments and hip-hop concerts.

Self-esteem Contentment with one's virtues and limitations; a blessed state that perpetually eludes those who chase after it. The dangling carrot that drives the self-help industry.

Self-help An American industry founded on the premise that most people are miserable being themselves and would gladly pay any number of authors, psychologists and mountebanks who hold out the promise of becoming somebody else.

Semiotics The philosophical study of signs and symbols; Latin for "Sounds impressive but we're just putting you on, folks."

Yet another lofty Eurodiscipline created for the express purpose of gratifying academic *poseurs* in turtlenecks. See also EXISTENTIALISM.

SENILITY The pleasantly rueful experience of forgetting what we've forgotten; a cleansing of the mental blackboard shortly before class is dismissed.

SENIOR CITIZENS Mellow survivors honored by traditional cultures for their accumulated wisdom; admired in America as long as they're sufficiently spunky and hot to trot; i.e., as long as they remind us of *young* people.

SENSITIVITY TRAINING An incubator from which fledgling touchy-feelies are released into society.

SENTIMENTALITY (archaic) A sweet sadness that would descend upon the Victorian mind, esp. when contemplating some object of affection irretrievably lost; the taboo emotion of the modern era.

SEQUEL Evidence that more is usually too much.

SERIAL KILLER A hunter, dictator, butterfly collector or anyone else whose hobby is the extermination of life.

SEX-CHANGE OPERATION Surgical transformation of an extroverted body into an introverted one, or vice versa; the ultimate gesture in the quest for self-improvement.

SEXUALITY One's bedroom demeanor worn outside the bedroom, like a badge or a hairdo to be admired by curious onlookers. Although it is commonly suspected that Americans engaged in sex before the 1960s, it appears to have been a well-kept secret, at least among white middle-class Protestants; as far as we know, Susan B. Anthony and Luther Burbank never discussed their *amours* on talk shows. Since the 1960s public personalities have tended increasingly to be *pubic* personalities.

SHALLOWNESS The root cause of chronic good health, high school popularity, appearance on the fiction best-seller lists and gainful employment on local TV news broadcasts. A most useful commodity, especially in combination with a pretty face.

SHAVE What trendy young men do each morning to simulate the appearance of a three-day growth.

SHOPPING MALL The marketplace that killed Main Street; a synthetic conglomeration of shops and teenagers reproduced along more or less identical lines throughout the North American continent, so that intelligent visitors may experience the same chill of alienation wherever their travels take them.

SHOULDER PADS The part of a football player's uniform designed to make him look as fearsome as a female executive.

SIDE EFFECTS Symptoms of a cure that induce nostalgia for the original disease.

SINGLE Unshackled, uncompromising, unfulfilled.

SINGLES BAR An after-hours watering hole for unattached sales reps, secretaries, junior execs and other kindred spirits, who flock there to engage in mutually satisfying sexual harassment.

SITCOM What network television does best: put witticisms in the mouths of performing yuppies and remind us when to laugh.

SKID ROW The nightmarish back alley of the American Dream;

153

an address shared by those who have slipped off the proverbial ladder of success and hit the pavement with a resounding thud.

SKIING   The not unpleasant spectacle of upwardly mobile folks heading rapidly downhill while clad in polyester. Those who reel at the prospect of sliding down a mountainside may take a quick shortcut to the festivities at the lodge, where nobody will be the wiser.

SLANG   Today's cutting-edge code words; tomorrow's dated clichés. The jargon of adolescent insiders, adolescent pseudo-insiders, pseudo-adolescent insiders, pseudo-adolescent pseudo-insiders and jazz musicians; a slithery vocabulary that changes its skin regularly to elude the grasp of undesirables such as parents and compilers of dictionaries.

Example:

(1950s)	*cool*
(1960s)	*groovy; far out*
(1970s)	*funky*
(1980s)	*awesome; excellent*
(1990s)	*cool*

SLEAZE   The raw material used by the mass media to manufacture instant celebrities and the made-for-TV movies that immortalize them; a slimy substance currently more profitable than petroleum or snake oil.

SLOGANS   Popular catchphrases repeated relentlessly in Communist nations to promote Marxist ideology and in the West to sell toothpaste.

Smile   To expose a portion of one's skeleton as a gesture of goodwill toward a fellow human; also a sign of amusement, esp. at the misfortunes of our rivals, as well as an involuntary twitch that tells a more powerful person we'll eat just about anything.

Smile Button   The visual equivalent of ''Have a nice day''; a wanton assault on the blissful misery of cynics.

Smirk   To smile secretly at one's ability to tell or understand in-jokes that baffle the polyester crowd. The self-satisfied face of contemporary American comedy.

Smoking   Voluntary self-pollution, still a favorite hobby among millions of enthusiasts with abbreviated life expectancies; once an almost compulsory adult pastime, imbued with the hard-boiled romance of big-city private eyes and lady spies in trench coats; now banned in public buildings by America's health police, forcing renegade hobbyists to take a whiff of fresh air along with the fatal weed.

Sneakers   The rubbery footwear cherished by hyperactive youth and pretenders to that status. The more prestigious varieties can cost nearly as much as a night in a hospital room, which is where numerous inner-city youngsters pass the time after refusing to surrender their favorite pair.

Snobbery   The belief among the upper classes that all members of the lower classes are louts; the corresponding belief among the lower classes that all members of the upper classes are twits.

Soap Opera An open-ended televised chronicle of sex and pettiness among the well-to-do, known to ensnare the unfortunate addict for a lifetime of wretched dependence. The bastard offspring of the nineteenth-century serial novel, scaled down to better reflect the tastes and aspirations of a postliterate audience.

Soccer The primary excuse for rioting in nations other than the U.S.

Social Register Dial-a-Deb.

Social Security An allowance paid to retired workers in inverse proportion to their need, so that the poor among them might spend the rest of their lives dining on dog food. As the elderly population booms and funds dwindle, everyone may be compelled to eat tree bark.

Social Workers Altruistic souls who renounce wealth for the opportunity to engage in lively repartee with irate poor people.

Socialism Transformation of the state into a milquetoast Robin Hood, a pudgy gray bureaucrat who robs from the spirit to give to the poor.

Sociobiology The cynic's science, based on the theory that the individual man, orangutan or sea cucumber is simply a convenient mechanism for ensuring the survival of ancient and dictatorial genes.

Software Information designed to be played back as programmed; bears roughly the same relationship to a computer as a record to a phonograph or *Das Kapital* to a diehard Marxist, except that software is interactive.

Space A vastness beyond the gravitational pull of Planet Earth, currently occupied by celestial bodies and habitués of new-age crystal shops.

Space Exploration The grand adventure that permanently lost some of its popular appeal when the surface of Mars was revealed to look like Nevada sans casinos or Wayne Newton.

Specialization A narrow professional excellence attained by the use of intellectual blinders; obsession made profitable.

Speed Limit The velocity one must exceed by approximately 10 mph on a major highway or risk being run off the road.

Speeding Propelling oneself forward at a pace that increases the likelihood of a crack-up, esp. as practiced by businesspeople who are expected to produce sixteen hours of work in an eight-hour day.

Sperm Bank A catalog store that enables mateless women to order designer genes for their children, typically from a broad selection of Nobel laureates, rock stars, wealthy sheet-metal contractors and other prestigious manufacturers. The means by which men have planted the seed of their own obsolescence.

Sports A religion whose fanatical followers worship a god named Jock.

Sportsman What a hunter calls himself when he slaughters animals for amusement as opposed to need.

Sprouts Innocent green plants snatched in their infancy and devoured alive by ravenous vegetarians.

Spy Thriller A cold-war Western with an impossibly convoluted plot designed to impress the reader with his or her own feeblemindedness; a once-popular form of entertainment now destined to go the way of the Soviet Union.

Stand-up Comic Personal essayist for the postliterate era; a glib and audacious fellow who must lie about his experiences in a manner that generates repetitive convulsive spasms in the diaphragms of his patrons.

Star A performer who makes more than his or her agent.

Also: **Superstar** A performer who makes more than Guatemala.

State Trooper A stealthy roadside predator whose prospective victims elude him by slowing down en masse, generally from 15 mph over the speed limit to 15 mph below.

State-of-the-art Soon-to-be-obsolete.

Status Symbol The right car, wristwatch, dog or polo shirt; any esteemed possession worn as a badge of superiority so that the wearer will not be forced to prove such status in a test of wits or character.

Stereotype A shoe designed to fit all feet within a particular ethnic or social group. When the shoe actually fits, as it sometimes will, the satisfied salesmen exchange sly winks across the room.

STERILE Incapable of generating life, like a man with a vasectomy or any building in a suburban office park.

STEROIDS Illicit hormones used by do-or-die athletes to pump themselves up until they burst; a latter-day version of Faust's bargain with the Devil, who delivers the victories but eventually comes to collect a bigger trophy.

STIGMA A moral tattoo that used to be etched onto unwed mothers and similar wayward types, effectively deterring others from the same path until tattoos became fashionable.

STOCK MARKET A popular game of chance in which moneyed speculators gamble with the nation's economy, the object being to amass as much unearned income as possible before one's fellow gamblers withdraw from the game and precipitate a nationwide depression.

STOCKBROKER Bookie to the speculating class; a friendly persuader who, if he listened to his own advice, would now be lounging on skid row.

STREET GANG A territorial pack of young urban wolves whose members provide a valuable public service by eliminating their rivals on a regular basis.

STREET LOONIES Generally the only big-city inhabitants a stranger may count on for honest conversation.

STREET SMARTS The key to success in most human endeavors; something we neglected to learn in school because we were too busy studying French and trigonometry.

Stress Collective term for the insults a body must endure when thrust into a less-than-congenial predicament; e.g., overwork, unemployment, a shopping mall in December or a vacation with one's in-laws. An effective antidote to the increased life expectancy made possible by recent advances in medical science.

Stretch Limo An elongated chauffeur-driven apparatus, generally exceeding the length of an adult *stegosaurus,* that proclaims the importance of its passengers while concealing their actual identities from the stares of the unwashed.

Strike When union workers take an open-ended vacation, all at the same time, in an attempt to win sympathy from management.

Strip Mining A monumental form of outdoor sculpture in which the artist carves deep parallel ridges into the sides of mountains, creating a series of bold horizontals enhanced by natural chiaroscuro lighting.

Stud A slut with chest hair.

Subculture The basic unit of clannishness in post-ethnic, post-religious, post geographic America, enabling an Irish Catholic from Cleveland to forge a bold new identity as a ballroom-dancing champion or an Amway representative.

Subsidy An allowance the federal government pays unmarried women who produce bountiful crops and farmers who don't. Some agriculturists actually receive money on the condition they produce nothing at all, a practice that would better serve society if extended to cigarette manufacturers and rap artists.

Suburbia   A scattered archipelago of residential enclaves offering neither the diversions of city life nor the rustic solace of the countryside; a world characterized by a comforting blandness of architecture and mental outlook, which may explain why it has lured a statistical majority of the American populace.

Success   Personal salvation as pursued by the American go-getter; an elusive commodity that, when finally attained, usually finds the achiever too exhausted and atherosclerotic to enjoy it.

Suicide, Assisted   The peculiar need, possible only in an over-professionalized society, to entrust a final act of private desperation to a qualified expert.

Suicide, Teenage   A young bird that hurls itself from the nest because it looks at its stubby wings and despairs of ever being able to fly.

Sunbelt   A land of perpetual summer that stretches from Disneyland to Disney World, its two main cultural centers. Now attracting hordes of new settlers as winter-weary Yankees forsake home and history for a chance to mow the lawn twelve months a year.

Sunglasses   Shaded spectacles worn outdoors by the overheated and indoors by the oppressively cool.

Sunspots   Small dark areas that may indicate turbulence on the sun or malignant melanoma on those who stay out in it too long.

Supermarket   The grocery store that made grocers obsolete. A prodigious pantry stocked with enough varieties of breakfast cereal to cause acute nervous disorders in sensitive shoppers, esp. those lately arrived from Third World nations. See also CHECKOUT COUNTER.

Supermarket Tabloid   A compact journal filled with tall tales of celebrity infidelities, woes, gaffes, feuds and diseases, so as to minimize mass resentment of their undeserved fame and wealth. Proof positive that the public rewards those who insult its intelligence in an entertaining manner.

Support Group   The company that misery loves; a club formed by those whose suffering takes a specialized form, like Tengmalm's syndrome or a crippling fear of badgers, and whose members derive deep comfort from knowing that somebody in the room is even worse off than they are.

Surfing   An imported California water sport that apparently turns the hair blond and reduces the vocabulary of its adherents to approximately twenty words, half of which are *dude*.

Surgery   The attempted repair, removal, replacement or rearrangement of uncooperative innards, occasionally necessitating the disposal of the patient (see MALPRACTICE).

Survivalist   A future-minded citizen who looks forward to the day, post-Armageddon, when he can take aim at the neighbors who pound desperately at his door.

Suspenders   Over-the-shoulder straps used to keep the pants of preschoolers from falling down; a fashion statement widely imitated by fast-track corporate climbers.

SYCOPHANTS Shameless subordinates who earn their sustenance by courting and flattering the powerful, like those scrawny birds that live by plucking food particles from the teeth of crocodiles. A species frequently sighted in Hollywood studios, New York ad agencies and corporate boardrooms across America.

T-SHIRT A portable personal billboard, emblazoned with a suitable commercial logo or message that creates an instant identity for the wearer and proclaims it to the world; in its unadorned state, considered an article of underwear.

TABOO Any strict cultural prohibition that, when breached, causes everyone in the group to gasp; e.g., cannibalism, public nudity, serving fried pork rinds at a Hasidic wedding, or an-

swering the question How are you? in the negative. See also
ENVELOPE, PUSHING THE.

Talk Show A televised opportunity for people to confess to
millions of viewers what they would be ashamed to admit to
their next-door neighbors.

Tanning An attempt by pale Nordics to approximate the rich
native hue of Arabs and Hispanics, with the results ranging
from lobster red to burnt orange to light pink with ominous
brown speckles.

Target Marketing A selling strategy that succeeds by staking
a small claim and mining it to the hilt; e.g., advertising in a
magazine aimed at affluent male backpackers between the ages
of thirty-five and forty-nine who live in Delaware and play the
kazoo at pet funerals.

Tattoo Lurid images of skulls, spiders, red hearts and unicorns
permanently drilled into the burning flesh of motorbikers and
other primitives, who actually pay to become walking repositor-
ies of the world's worst art. A recent trend is to decorate parts
of the body generally concealed from public view, adding an
intriguing new twist to the age-old invitation to "come over
and see my etchings."

Tax Revolt A defiant gesture by folks who gladly eat at Uncle
Sam's Diner but resent having to pick up the check.

Teacher Hardworking host of a daytime talk show, sadly underpaid by show-business standards and frequently tuned out by

large portions of the audience, some of whom might be forced to spend the following year watching reruns.

TEACHING ASSISTANT A young scholar assigned by major universities to explain difficult subjects to undergraduates, preferably in an impenetrable foreign accent.

TECHNOCRACY The nerd's utopia: a society in which a technological elite controls the machines, and the machines control everybody else.

TEENAGER An oddly proportioned creature propelled by hormones, prone to unsightly skin eruptions and given to a variety of mindless pastimes; in short, the human animal in its healthiest state.

TELEVANGELIST A charismatic good ol' boy with the power to perform miracles, such as transforming the donations of dirt-poor believers into a thirty-room mansion with a pink limousine out front.

TELEVISION An electronic breast that has suckled and comforted most of the civilized world, offering the illusion of human companionship without the attendant risks and disappointments—or the nuisance of compiling actual personal memories.

TEMPORARY INSANITY The plea of a tattooing victim the morning after, or of a small investor who just sank seven thousand dollars into yet another doomed penny stock.

TEMPS Migrant workers in business clothes.

TENNIS A socially acceptable outlet for the ferocity of white suburban achievers, who must work even when they play, must compete feverishly even in the presence of friends, must not only beat an opponent but reduce him to a quivering pile of gelatinous pulp, while in the distance the birds make melody and the summer breezes beckon.

TERM PAPER An opportunity for today's collegians to pick up potentially useful business techniques; e.g., subcontracting a job to qualified professionals and putting one's name to the ideas of others.

TERMINATION Corporate euphemism for involuntary cessation of employment; firing; sacking; banishment from the land of the living. ''And cast the unprofitable servant into outer darkness: there shall be weeping and gnashing of teeth'' (Mat. 25:30).

TERRORIST **1.** An armed fanatic who blows up innocent people in an attempt to enlist public sympathy for an obscure cause. **2.** A toddler on the loose. **3.** The parent of a child star. **4.** A grown child who writes an unauthorized biography of a famous parent.

THERMODYNAMICS, SECOND LAW OF The natural tendency of all things to deteriorate and get messy over time: civilizations, relationships, ripe bananas, tidy apartments or human bodies.

THIRD WORLD Popular geopolitical term of dubious etymology, as its perpetrators still balk at revealing the identities of the First and Second Worlds. Describes any nation whose entire middle class can fit comfortably aboard a large passenger ship, and in some cases already has.

THRILL SPORTS   Any of the climbing, flying, gliding, jumping, speeding, diving or neck-breaking pastimes pursued by an intense breed of quasi-professional experts, who repeatedly risk death to savor the same jolt of electricity some of us feel when we spot a white-winged crossbill at the bird feeder.

TIME BOMB   An explosive device set to detonate in the very near future, like an unmarried male subscriber to *Nazi Life* who has just been dismissed from his warehouse job at Mad Manny's Appliances. See also POSTAL WORKER.

TOKEN   Lone representative of a disadvantaged group, brought in to quash rumors of discrimination; e.g., a white player on a professional basketball squad.

TOLLBOOTH   A manmade bottleneck installed at the entrance to major highways, bridges and tunnels, causing us to drum on the dashboard while we observe the Cynic's Law of Line Selection ("The line one chooses at a tollbooth or supermarket checkout is invariably the slowest, regardless of its apparent length"), along with Corollary A ("If the line one chooses is not already the slowest, it automatically becomes so as soon as one chooses it") and Corollary B ("The amount of time one must wait in line varies in direct proportion to the urgency with which one must pass through it").

TOUCHY-FEELY   A personal space invader.

TOUPEE   A hairy fig leaf for a naked pate.

TRACT HOMES   Suburban domiciles built in mass quantities along virtually identical lines, for middle-class families who lead virtually identical lives. Formerly produced at low cost; always produced at the expense of the landscape.

TRAFFIC LIGHTS   Metaphor for the periodic stops and starts along the highway of our ambitions; commonly rigged, as in life itself, so that the driver who hits one red light hits them all.

TRAILER PARKS   Latter-day gypsy camps scattered throughout the vast American hinterland; humble places of abode where aspirations die young and tornadoes gravitate like flies to roadkill.

TRAIN   The most civilized, comfortable, romantic and therefore obsolescent means of public transport.

TRANQUILIZER   The opiate of the middle classes, prescribed as a remedy for anxiety, melancholia, chronic facial tics and other perfectly rational responses to modern urbanized society.

TRASH COMPACTOR   A powerful piece of equipment that crushes unwieldy refuse into neat little cubes; might someday be used to conserve space in our cemeteries.

TRASHY   Utterly devoid of wholesomeness but not without a certain sleazy appeal, like a spandex-clad Siren luring us to our ruin. Describes most daytime TV, supermarket tabloids, pop music, teenage hair statements, heavy-metal T-shirts, tattoos, kung fu films—in fact nearly everything in contemporary American culture that is not either boring or pretentious.

TREADMILL   The central feature of a stress test or a nine-to-five job, capable of precipitating a heart attack in either situation.

TRINITY   The traditional threefold divinity worshiped by ambitious Americans: money, sex and power. Now apparently superseded by a new *octinity:* money, sex, power, youth, fitness, low cholesterol, tight buns and lifelong therapy.

Troops Expendable male bodies sent by the U.S. to stop bullets during obscure foreign uprisings.

Trust Fund A lifetime on the private dole, thoughtfully arranged by Daddy so that Binky and Muffy might avoid the *public* one.

Truth The blinding light that causes so many of us to wear sunglasses indoors and out.

Tumor A mass of cells that grows haphazardly and serves no discernible purpose. See also BUREAUCRACY.

UFO's Elusive flying machines thought to be piloted by extra-terrestrials and generally confined in their earthly encounters to areas where the *National Enquirer* is considered a literary magazine.

UNDERACHIEVER Upper-middle-class euphemism for "hope-less," applied to those mildly embarrassing offspring who would rather become Taoist monks than investment bankers or dermatologists.

UNDERCLASS A chronically unfortunate segment of the population thought to lack all useful skills, except for a prodigious ability to increase its numbers.

UNDERDOG 1. A dachshund, corgi or chihuahua. 2. A seriously disadvantaged combatant, like a bespectacled podiatrist in a boxing ring, who invariably gains the inner fortitude and moral support required to become the overdog—at least in the minds of Hollywood screenwriters.

UNDERGROUND PRESS Collective term for those scruffy crusading publications that exist in a time warp where all the calendars have been stopped at 1969. Such periodicals typically cater to environmentally committed left-wing holistic vegetarian backpackers living in solar-heated wigwams, which explains why their circulations rarely approach that of, say, *Beverage Distributor Weekly*.

UNEMPLOYMENT The usual alternative to overwork. A full-time job that depletes energy and morale even more effectively than one's former occupation.

UNEXAMINED LIFE According to Socrates, the kind of life not worth living; a remark uttered in rebuke to Plato shortly after the latter gentleman returned from a wild week at Club Med.

UNIFORMS Lookalike apparel (e.g., football jerseys, army khaki, monks' robes and business suits) donned by team players so as to minimize whatever remains of their former identities.

UNION An exclusive club for manual laborers, esp. those with well-placed in-laws. Formerly the socialist underbelly of the

American corporation; now notable for having transformed burly blue-collar workers into staunch conservatives with a patch of lawn to keep impeccably trimmed and weeded.

UNWED MOTHER One who helps perpetuate the genes of an unwed father, without the latter's talent for becoming invisible at will. A condition that sinks poor women deeper into poverty, while the unwed mothers of Hollywood tend to grow even more bankable.

UPPER CLASS The hereditary gentry worshiped by F. Scott Fitzgerald in a bygone age; aristocratic guardians of the gracious life, largely descended from nineteenth-century robber barons, slave owners, profiteers, fur traders, oilmen or dry-goods merchants.

UPPER MIDDLE CLASS An ambitious social caste recognized by the tendency of its members to adorn their homes with museum reproductions, their car windows with decals from high-ticket colleges, their bodies with designer labels and their stomachs with ulcers.

UPWARD MOBILITY An increasingly arduous struggle to exceed the socioeconomic status of one's parents, or, failing that, to acquire a taste for bottled mineral water and radicchio.

URBAN RENEWAL The replacement of old inner-city slums with newer, uglier ones.

URINAL The one place where all men are peers.

VACATION Cramming a year's worth of living into a period of approximately two weeks, in an attempt to relax from the rigors of work.

VALUES The debased coin of our times: solid silver replaced by a cheesy nickel-and-copper facsimile.

VAMPIRE A pale and sinister stalker who gains sustenance by sucking the blood of the living (see BOSS), thereby transforming them into kindred souls (see CONVERTS) who must spend the rest of eternity in search of fresh warm bodies (see PYRAMID SCHEME). Vampirical analysis suggests that if one of the undead were to bite a different victim each night, by the end of a single month the entire population of China would be wearing capes. One may elude the fangs of these fiends by brandishing a crucifix or hiding in an Italian kitchen.

VASECTOMY The unkindest cut; how a few brave men avoid having to face the local pharmacist on a Saturday night.

VCR An electronic device for capturing the flotsam of the airwaves and granting it an immortality denied to saints and sages.

VEGETARIAN An herbivorous individual with Buddhist tendencies. One who rejects the ghoulish concept of forking animal remains down the gullet, preferring to dine upon the corpses of plants and their detachable reproductive organs (popularly known as ''fruit'').

Also: **VEGAN** A vegetarian from another planet.

VENEER A thin, finely finished exterior that effectively conceals the underlying substance; e.g., a mortician's smile or the civility that prevails at a Hollywood party.

VENEREAL DISEASE Quaint generic term for sexually transmitted pestilences, dating to a time when the worst they could do was cause chancres and terminal insanity.

VIDEO CAMERA An audiovisual recording device thrust into the hands of the public so that future social historians might develop migraines looking at our school pageants, pet tricks, weddings and birthings.

Video Game   An electronic form of opium, consumed by stony-eyed young addicts either at home or in dark communal dens, where their families occasionally must venture to retrieve them.

Video Screen   A window without a view, gazed upon for hours on end by the most intelligent species ever to inhabit the earth. Successor to the printed page, the illuminated manuscript, the papyrus scroll, the hieroglyphic relief and the cave drawing as the primary source of second-hand information; doubtless to be replaced someday by three-dimensional images of men and women huddled around a fire, telling stories into the night.

Violence   An assault on personal property and body parts regarded as a means of self-expression; a surplus American commodity that ranks as one of our most popular cultural exports.

Virgin   A young innocent who in former times was sacrificed to the gods but who now merely lives in disgrace.

Virtual Reality   A much-hyped wonderland one can enter without falling down a rabbit hole, although you would be hard pressed to encounter anything as substantial as a Cheshire cat or as merry as a mad tea-party.

Virtue   A quality of quiet saintliness that today incites even more resentment than undeserved wealth or success at Trivial Pursuit.

Vitamins   Chunky little pills that may extend our lives if they don't lodge in our throats.

Vocational School   A humble educational establishment that trains the manually inclined for an assortment of useful dead-end careers, most of which pay better than teaching at a vocational school.

VOICE MAIL   Yet another technological convenience that enables us to avoid close encounters with real people.

VOTING   The right of our citizens to do as they please behind a curtain, as long as they do it alone.

WAKE **1.** A convivial soiree with a preserved corpse in the room. **2.** What the mourners would be visibly startled to see the corpse do, esp. those expecting a sizable inheritance.

WAR One of the more popular televised spectator sports, despite the notable lack of coherent scoring rules and genial play-by-play commentary.

WEDDING A religious ceremony commonly followed by a catered extravaganza featuring chopped-liver sculpture and accordion bands. A good time had by all at the expense of the bride's father; the reason most married men still pray for sons.

WEDDING RING   A subtle signal to single admirers that they should abandon all hope, since the wearer already has.

WEIGHT LIFTER   One who, if his body were a car, would design himself along the lines of a 1959 Cadillac.

WELFARE   A public safety net strung up in the 1960s to catch the casualties of the free market system and keep them tangled in the webbing for generations.

WEREWOLF   A legendary predator prone to monthly bouts of FMS (Full Moon Syndrome), which, like the more mundane monthly affliction observed in human females, have been known to trigger wanton attacks on the innocent—with the added embarrassment of rapid hair growth and a serious underbite that defies the efforts of the best orthodontists.

WESTERN CIVILIZATION   (archaic) The reviled culture of Dead White European Males; notable for having survived the onslaughts of Visigoths, Vandals and Vikings, only to sputter out unlamented during the age of Video. Spurned by enlightened academics who find it insufficient as a means of promoting their political agenda. Unpopular, too, among those who sense their shortcomings all the more acutely in the presence of the sublime. Still recognized by some authorities for having made a few notable contributions to the advancement of our species; e.g., flying buttresses, forks, bifocals and whitewall tires.

WETLANDS The marshy wilderness frequented by ducks, the hunters who shoot them, the environmentalists who lecture the hunters, and the condominium developers who inevitably outfox them all.

WHITE-COLLAR CRIME A reprehensible greed-related offense that generally lands the perpetrator in an exclusive country club. See MINIMUM SECURITY PRISON.

WHITE SUPREMACISTS The most convincing argument against the theory of white racial superiority.

WILDERNESS AREA Primary source of the raw material for junk mail, supermarket tabloids, romance novels, user's manuals, toilet tissue and this dictionary.

WILDLIFE MANAGEMENT The periodic massacre of formerly endangered animals that have lately enjoyed unexpected success in their amorous activities.

WIMP Another of society's terms of abuse for a gentle man.

WINE Aged grape juice regarded as a collectible by American connoisseurs, and foolishly consumed by Europeans for the mellow glow that it is said to impart.

WIRETAP A form of electronic eavesdropping that kept FBI officials entertained in the era before telephone-sex hot lines.

WITCH-HUNT An often brutal investigation carried out with the intention of rounding up social and political subversives; a technique loudly decried because it tends to capture more friends-of-witches than witches.

WOMEN'S STUDIES The academic discipline devoted to an emerging ethnic group noted for quaint folk traditions like needlepoint and witchcraft.

WORKAHOLIC Someone addicted to a hallucinogen called workahol, which grotesquely distorts the importance of one's efforts at the office and shrinks everything else—earth, ocean, art, poetry, love, music, wine, watermelon and chronic domestic squabbles—into pale and permanent irrelevance.

WORKING CLASS Those who labor in the bowels of American industry, assuming they can still find a bowel that will employ them; sturdy, genial, beer-drinking folk whose personal value system would never allow them to set foot in a fern bar.

WRINKLES Telltale creases notable for diminishing the market value of baseball cards and news anchorwomen, while exercising the opposite effect on sportswear and anchormen.

WRISTWATCH A fashion accessory with a clock in the middle, its status value being roughly proportional to the illegibility of the dial.

WRITERS' WORKSHOP A summer camp attended by aspiring authors in the hope of discovering their "true voice," which, in all likelihood, will emerge as a small, reedy instrument similar in timbre, pitch and volume to the voices of their instructors and fellow campers.

X-chromosome A genetic double cross that empowers women with the ability to bear children and reserves for men the right to be color-blind hemophiliacs.

Xenophobia A pervasive fear and loathing of anything foreign, commonly voiced by Americans of European ancestry as they dine on pork lo mein while enjoying Arnold Schwarzenegger on their Japanese VCRs.

X-ray A diagnostic tool used to detect existing cancerous growths and create new ones for future examinations to reveal.

Y-CHROMOSOME A line of genes designed for men only; the cause of virility, war, baldness, hockey, sex crimes, clever inventions and a disinclination to ask for directions when lost.

YACHT The stretch limo of the seas.

YAHOOS Ignorant savages characterized by a pronounced lack of taste and intellectual capacity; e.g., critics of this dictionary.

YOGURT A thriving colony of bacteria swimming in curdled milk; a pleasantly sour concoction said to extend the life spans of Caucasian mountain-folk, at least when consumed in conjunction with fresh air, vigorous goat-chasing and a stress-free work environment. Popular in the U.S., esp. among dieters, who enjoy it laced with sugar and preserves.

Youth The too-brief span wherein the human chassis is factory-fresh, undented and free of corrosion; a pristine condition worshiped by menopausal women in sweatsuits and shrinking men with chestnut-brown toupees, while those who actually possess it are frequently too shallow or despondent to appreciate it.

Yuppie A young and fluid creature, generally wanting in identity, that succeeds by studiously mimicking the members of its species that have already succeeded. Locally abundant in the fashionable districts of most cities, where it commonly travels about in small self-regarding packs; prime specimens may be viewed at the trendiest restaurants, dining happily on esoteric pastas accompanied by sun-dried tomatoes and balsamic vinegar.

Zipper Two rows of unsmiling teeth that often induce laughter in others, esp. when inadvertently left open following a trip to the john.

Zombie One of the walking dead; a mirthless creature beloved by teenage horror-movie fans and those in charge of hiring at accounting firms.

Zoning Local ordinances that typically prohibit commercial construction adjacent to bird sanctuaries or family dwellings, at least until a wealthy developer proposes a $500 million shopping mall for the site.

Zoo A pleasant and instructive wildlife park, lately denounced for depriving animals of their right to starve or be eaten alive in their natural habitats.

Zzzzzz The sound produced by those who have attempted to read this entire dictionary at one sitting.